AWAKENED:

CHANGE YOUR MINDSET TO TRANSFORM YOUR TEACHING

SECOND EDITION

Also by Angela Watson:

Fewer Things, Better:
The Courage to Focus on What Matters Most
(2019)

Unshakeable:
20 Ways to Enjoy Teaching Every Day...No Matter What
(2015)

The Awakened Devotional Guide for
Christian Educators
(2012; No Longer in Print)

Awakened:
Change Your Mindset to Transform Your Teaching
(2011; First Edition, No Longer in Print)

The Cornerstone:
Classroom Management That Makes Teaching
More Effective, Efficient, and Enjoyable
(2009, No Longer in Print)
See programs at 40htw.com for continually
updated resources on this topic

AWAKENED:

CHANGE YOUR MINDSET TO TRANSFORM YOUR TEACHING

SECOND EDITION

ANGELA WATSON

Awakened: Change Your Mindset to Transform Your Teaching
by Angela Watson

Names and identifying details have been changed to protect the
anonymity of persons and events mentioned herein.

Published by Due Season Press and Educational Services.

ISBN-13: 978-0-9823127-5-9
ISBN-10: 0-9823127-15-X

Printed in the United States of America.

Second Edition

This book is dedicated to teachers everywhere who wonder,
"Is it just me?"

It's not just you—I promise.

I'd especially like to dedicate this book to the Truth for Teachers and 40 Hour Teacher Workweek communities. You believed in my vision and made it your own, creating change on a level I could never make by myself. Your enthusiasm, support, and passion have played an enormous role in making this book possible. Thank you for inspiring me with the work you do each day in your schools and spreading the word about my resources.

Thanks also to Kali Engelbert and Monica Macareg for helping bringing this book—and everything I create for teachers—into existence; and to Jennifer Gonzalez and my husband, Curtis, for your endless wisdom, patience, and guidance. All four of you were an important part of the last book and stuck with me through this one, too. I'm eternally grateful for that.

Definitions

Some terms in Awakened may be new to you, while other terms have different meanings to different people. Here's a brief definition of my understanding of each of the main approaches you'll find woven into this book. For sources, I've chosen online articles with easily-accessible, layperson language. Links to each source and other recommended resources can be found at TruthforTeachers.com/awakened.

Mind-Body Connection:
The belief that the causes, development and outcomes of a physical illness are determined from the interaction of psychological, social, and biological factors. It's important to note that "mind" is not synonymous with brain. Instead, in our definition, the mind consists of mental states such as thoughts, emotions, beliefs, attitudes, and images. The brain is the hardware that allows us to experience these mental states. *(Source: Taking Charge by the University of Minnesota)*

Mindfulness:
The basic human ability to be fully present, aware of where we are and what we're doing, and not overly reactive or overwhelmed by what's going on around us. Mindfulness is a quality that every human being already possesses. It's not something you have to conjure up, you just have to learn how to access it. While mindfulness is innate, it can be cultivated through proven techniques. *(Source: Mindful.org)*

Acceptance and commitment therapy (ACT):
An empirically based psychological intervention that uses acceptance and mindfulness along with commitment and behavior-change strategies to increase psychological flexibility. The objective of ACT is not elimination of difficult feelings; rather, it is to be present with what life brings and to "move toward valued behavior." ACT invites people

to open up to unpleasant feelings, learn not to overreact to them, and not avoid situations where they are invoked. Its therapeutic effect aims to be a positive spiral where a greater understanding of one's emotions leads to a better understanding of the truth. In ACT, truth is measured through the concept of workability, or what works to take another step toward what matters, e.g., values, meaning. *(Source: Psychology Today)*

Cognitive behavioral therapy (CBT)
A type of psychotherapeutic treatment that helps people learn how to identify and change the destructive or disturbing thought patterns that have a negative influence on their behavior and emotions. Through CBT, faulty thoughts are identified, challenged, and replaced with more objective, realistic thoughts. *(Source: Verywellmind.com)*

Dialectical Behavior Therapy (DBT)
A newer type of CBT that addresses destructive or disturbing thoughts and behaviors while incorporating treatment strategies of emotional regulation and mindfulness. The term "dialectical" comes from the idea that bringing together two opposites in therapy -- acceptance and change -- brings better results than either one alone. *(Source: WebMD)*

This book draws upon my lived experiences and curation of the most helpful approaches of each practice above through a trauma-informed lens for educators. I'll offer a wide variety of tools so you can decide when and how to use each approach.

Table of Contents

PART ONE:
SETTING THE FOUNDATION FOR A HEALTHY MIND

PART TWO:
CREATING NEW MENTAL PATTERNS

PART THREE:
CULTIVATING A HEALTHY MINDSET

Preface to the second edition: what's changed (and why)

The toughest part of writing a book—at least in my experience—is the finality of it all.

When my thinking changes about something I explore in a blog article, podcast episode, or social media post, I can add an update or disclaimer. I can change it, delete it, or post a follow-up.

But a book requires me to be *really, really sure* about an idea and my explanation of it before putting it out into the world. Printed copies of the first edition of this book are forever, and still remain in tens of thousands of homes and classrooms all over the world.

And yet...if I wait to publish until I'm absolutely certain that I know *everything* there is to know about a topic and I'm 100% positive that the information will never change, then obviously I'd never write any books. Some works age better than others, but there's no way to write a book on teaching or mindset that won't eventually become dated.

Though I think many readers haven't considered it this way, every book is ultimately a snapshot in time. It captures the author's research and understanding within the context of their learning so far...and that learning continues every day that we're alive. Everything we create is a product of our time, lived experiences, and understandings.

All the authors I know regret some of the things they've put into print. Some wish they could change their wording in a certain spot, or add and remove specific examples. And for others, there's a concern that their work may be misused or create harm. Once you've released your ideas into the world, you no longer have control over them, and people will apply them in ways you never imagined (both positively and negatively.)

So when you have a long legacy of work--I started my teaching website in 2003--there will eventually come a time when you either put your head in the sand and ignore your old cringe-worthy stuff, or you deal with it.

In 2021, I decided to take my first book out of print. It was called *The Cornerstone: Classroom Management That Makes Teaching More Effective, Efficient, and Enjoyable,* and was published in 2009. Frankly, I don't want teachers buying classroom management advice that's well over a decade old, and there were a couple of chapters that I can see now are problematic and reinforce negative stereotypes.

When I pulled *The Cornerstone,* I'd already taken the most relevant parts of that book and developed the 40 Hour Teacher Workweek program. This is an online, self-paced course with downloadable resources, printables, audio resources, and more.

40 Hour has been available since 2015, and I have a team of people who check for outdated links and add more current resources every year. We also did a major overhaul to the entire program in 2020 to reflect pandemic teaching as well as user feedback about how I might

better organize and format the materials. I love creating online courses because I can add new resources as education changes and edit things as I grow both personally and professionally.

But with this book, *Awakened,* a second edition felt like the best way to update my ideas.

I wanted to create a new version of the book which reflects not only how the world has changed, but how my thinking has changed.

Looking back at the version of Awakened I first published in 2011, I can see three distinct phases in the path toward becoming who I am today. The first phase was driven largely by my understanding of the Bible and my Christian upbringing. The second phase was driven by cognitive-behavioral therapy and neuroscience.

Over the past few years, I've entered a new phase of personal development that's fueled by a more holistic mind-body approach. I've also explored how many of the problems we attribute to our own personal faults are actually coping mechanisms or learned behaviors. Our mental health is not developed in a bubble, and is greatly impacted by societal expectations as well as systemic and institutional structures.

Through all these stages of my personal development, I can see many common threads, and I think you'll notice them as you read this second edition.

This time around, the book is even more centered on non-attachment to expectations and outcomes, along with non-judgment toward yourself and others.

You'll find a heavy emphasis on letting go instead of trying harder; of unpacking behaviors and thought processes and releasing the ones that aren't serving you well.

The goal is to be the observer of your thoughts, and *choose* the perspectives that align with your values and how you want to feel. This includes building an awareness of our biases--including prejudice and stereotypes--but also confirmation bias, recency bias, and other things our brains do to help us stay alive that create all kinds of distorted, inaccurate thought patterns.

Radical acceptance is another running theme in the book: accepting what is, so you can work to make peace with, adapt to, or create needed change from a place of clear-headed insight. There are some parts of teaching (and life) for which cultivating a neutral emotional experience is probably the best-case scenario, and I share many healthy reframing strategies that *don't* aim for a positive outlook.

These were all principles in the first edition of the book that I've developed much more fully in the second.

So what's been removed?

I've taken out references to religion and spiritual practices that some folks found distracting and that no longer reflect my own beliefs. These mentions were intended to be inclusive but had the opposite effect in some cases, and prevented me from encouraging public schools to utilize the book with their teachers.

I've also removed or edited paragraphs that could be perceived as toxic positivity. I've been careful not to imply that if you're unhappy in teaching, it's your own fault, and that if you just think differently about your circumstances, everything will be great. You'll see more acknowledgment of the need for systemic change and tips for how to advocate for better working conditions without burning out.

Perhaps the biggest change is an acknowledgement of the mind-body connection, which frankly I didn't understand at all when I wrote the first edition. I heavily reworked multiple sections of the book to address listening to our bodies and intuition, and responding when feelings arise not from thoughts but from trauma that is stored in the body. While I'm not an expert on these realities yet, it felt important to acknowledge them and guide you toward other resources where you can learn more.

One of the best parts of creating this second edition has been seeing my own growth as a writer. I think you'll find this book flows better, has more natural and less stilted language, and explains concepts more clearly. At least, I hope so! I've had twelve additional years of regular writing and publishing experience since I wrote the first version of *Awakened*, and it's been rewarding to see how my voice as a writer has evolved.

I re-wrote this book in large part for myself: I wanted to once again feel comfortable having this book exist in the world with my name on it. But more so, of course, this book was written for YOU.

Teaching has not become an easier profession over the last decade. The COVID-19 pandemic created a roller coaster of unpredictable, uncertain, and unstable teaching and learning conditions which we are still recovering from. Currently we're seeing a greater number of teachers resign, retire, and walk out than ever before in my lifetime.

Changing the way you think cannot fix all the problems in education. But for those teachers who have decided to stay—or want to stay, or need to stay—your mindset is an aspect of your work that you have a great deal of control over.

Your mindset is worth attending to, so that you can live the best life available to you and show up as the best version of yourself for your students.

I kept the title and subtitle of this book the same, because I do still think of mindset work as an awakening. Each new "aha moment" and realization about what's working in my thought patterns (and what's not) brings me to a greater level of contentment and peace. *Awakened* is still a fitting title, because I want you to experience those moments of new insights and possibilities, too.

And, even though so many other things are different now than ten-plus years ago, I do still believe that changing your mindset can transform your teaching. More than that, it can transform the entire way you live your life and bring you into better alignment with who you really are.

Thanks for taking this journey with me, whether it's for the first time or several years after the first time you read *Awakened*.

This second edition is a snapshot of where I'm at right now…and I can only hope to have the kind of life experiences and personal growth that would lead me to write a third edition in another ten years.

This process of transforming our minds to live with full integrity and authenticity never ends. I'm glad you're here with me on the path.

Angela Watson
Brooklyn, NY
November 2022

PART ONE:

SETTING THE FOUNDATION FOR A HEALTHY MIND

Introduction:
How I learned everything the hard way

What personality traits does a teacher need to be successful and rise above the challenges of the profession? It's not hard to rattle off a reasonable list of qualities—patience, persistence, flexibility, and the right amount of empathy, perhaps. An effective teacher is not easily discouraged, maintains a positive outlook, and enjoys being with students. Pretty straightforward stuff, right?

As a new teacher, I found that displaying ANY of those qualities required a huge inner struggle.

I loved teaching and adored my kids, but the demands of the job wore me down quickly on most days. I was often extremely impatient. Constantly repeating myself for the students was agitating, and when they didn't do what I told them the very first time, I got frustrated.

Expressing that frustration created a stress response that raised my blood pressure and cortisol levels, but restraining myself and playing the role of a calm teacher depleted an inordinate amount of energy, too. Either way, the normal daily challenges that come with being around children often left me exhausted and cranky.

And it wasn't just the kids. Nothing frustrated me more than a sudden change in schedule or having another unnecessary and time-consuming responsibility piled onto my plate...and that was usually multiple times a day.

After school, I'd drag myself over to an equally disillusioned co-worker's classroom and together we'd bemoan how disorganized "the system" was. How could we possibly be expected to teach when we didn't have the supplies or planning time and there were too many kids crowded into a tiny, run-down classroom? I felt like it was my duty to fight against a dysfunctional system that put kids dead last in priority, and I did so by...well, complaining as much as possible.

I also had a skewed sense of empathy. I felt an unhelpful sense of pity toward my students, worrying endlessly about what I saw as their tragic home lives. And yet I held too little empathy for their families: I stood in a constant state of judgment, internally criticizing their capabilities each time they didn't show up for conferences or disciplined their children in ways that didn't fit my beliefs about the "best" way to parent. I still had a lot to learn about culturally responsive teaching and hadn't even begun to examine my savior mentality.

Needless to say, I was not a happy teacher.

That's not to say I was a *bad* teacher; my instructional methods and rapport with students were both solid. I rarely experienced conflicts with or complaints from families. My administrators raved that I was a natural, someone with "the gift." Just three months into my career during my first formal observation, the Pre-K program supervisor had asked me to become a demonstration teacher for the district and present some of my techniques at a county-wide workshop.

Right from the start, I had established a strong reputation for excellence: my kids were learning in leaps and bounds, and our classroom routines ran smoothly.

But. It took everything out of me to keep it that way, because what was happening on the inside of me was not aligned with what I was presenting on the outside.

Trying to maintain every aspect of a classroom with a friendly smile on my face was both physically and emotionally draining. I felt like an actor putting on a one-woman Broadway show (*"In this performance, Angela will play the part of a healthy, well-adjusted educator who loves her job!!"*) The audience clapped and cheered, but behind the scenes, I was a wreck.

There was no possible way I could keep that up until retirement…and the fact that I started counting down with just a few years under my belt was NOT a good sign.

Clearly, I needed either a change of career or perspective, but at that stage in my life, the latter never occurred to me. For my attitude to change, I assumed my circumstances needed to change.

So after just three years in the early childhood classroom, I spent the summer applying for federal government education jobs in Washington, D.C., where I lived. I envisioned myself sitting at a cushy desk in a private office with an endless supply of free sticky notes and no one calling my name endlessly in a tiny, high-pitched voice.

One day in late July that year, I went into a dollar store to pick up some things for the house and found myself drawn to the toy aisle out of habit. My eye went immediately to a package of bunny-shaped mini erasers that would make the most fabulous math manipulatives. I'd recently woken up in the middle of the night thinking of a super cool one-to-one correspondence game I could create, and those erasers would be the perfect addition!

As I held the materials in my hand, my heart sunk with the realization that I wouldn't have a classroom in which to use them. If I switched to a "normal" 9-5 job, I wouldn't have this particular outlet for my creativity. I would be letting go of my dream and my passion.

I knew in that moment I wasn't done teaching.

That fall, I transferred to a new school and moved up four grade levels. The change was exactly what I needed, and finding ways to meet the needs of a new age group completely renewed my enthusiasm for my work. I threw myself into creating a ton of activities, projects, and centers, and started my first website (*Ms. Powell's Management Ideas for Teachers*) to share my resources with others on a wider scale.

Over time I developed more savviness, and teaching became less tiring. But the stress of the job kept tugging me away from my vision; I had to fight constantly against the minor inconveniences and hassles that threatened to steal my enthusiasm over and over again.

No textbook or mentor had ever explained how to cope internally with the pressures that kept me from fully enjoying the job (and thereby kept me from sharing my enjoyment with students.)

I still spent too much time focusing on everything that was wrong, and one negative interaction in the morning could put me in a bad mood all day. My emotions were up and down, and I resented the fact that a bunch of nine-year-olds and one absent-minded principal had the ability to determine whether I had a good day or not.

Over the eleven years I was in the classroom, I taught in eight schools in three states. For the first half of my career, discouragement and disillusionment trailed behind me wherever I taught. I could delay it for a while by moving someplace new, but the problems in the next teaching position always managed to get me down.

Somehow I didn't make the connection that the common denominator in every school was *me*. I kept thinking the next school would be better, and once I realized that wasn't true, I figured it was the profession.

Yes, it was *education* that was the problem—I needed a new career!

Then I'd think back to the moment in the dollar store and remember that teaching was still my passion. So why was it so hard to stop being stressed and just *enjoy* it?

In November 2004, six years into my teaching career, I had an epiphany that changed my life forever. I'd moved to Miami that summer and was teaching a new grade level there, hoping to start fresh and have a better experience both personally and professionally than I'd had in the D.C. area. And yet I found myself still overwhelmed by frustration in every aspect of my life.

In the middle of a good old fashioned breakdown--crying on my bedroom floor--I realized that wherever I went, there I was. These issues were going to follow me no matter where I lived, what I taught, or whatever else was happening in my personal life.

The truth hit me like a bolt of lightning: *I had been continually changing my circumstances, but I'd never even attempted to change how I was showing up in my circumstances. It was my mindset and perspective that needed to change.*

This felt true not just in regard to teaching, but also in my personal life. Those self-defeating behaviors, habits, and negative thoughts had permeated every aspect of my existence. I had been running from myself, and I was finally willing to do the internal work I'd been avoiding.

From that day forward, I set out on a new spiritual and emotional path, steeping myself in personal development work. I learned that I didn't have to stay the way I was. I started to drop the excuses ("*Oh, it's just my personality—this is just the way I am*") and recognized that I could change not only the way I acted, but also the way I thought and felt.

Years later, I'd learn to see this as a letting go of the things I wasn't, rather than changing myself, but in the beginning of my personal development work, the idea of creating change felt empowering. Living inside my own mind could actually be a pleasant experience! I felt a sense of hope: I wasn't destined to be overwhelmed, stressed out, and discouraged every day of my life.

During the next five years—the last half of my career in the classroom—I explored many aspects of my personality that were working against me, and focused on developing a healthier outlook. And now as an instructional coach and educational consultant, I find myself still drawing on those lessons daily as I continue to shed the trauma, unhealthy habits, biases, and other baggage that no longer serve me. I've learned to stay focused on my vision and enjoy my work (and my life) in ways that were never possible when I was younger.

This process was not just about adequate sleep, exercise, healthy eating, and all those outward things that can help treat and prevent burnout: I'm talking about *inward* change.

This book is about lessons learned through my early years of frustration as well as the principles I discovered while seeking out a better path. I was fascinated by the amount of studies that scientifically *prove* we can decrease our stress and increase our contentment just by changing cognitive habits—and I think you'll be amazed, as well.

You'll also read about lessons I've been learning in recent years, such as how trauma is stored in the body and the importance of the mind/body connection. I believe now that *all* feelings are for feeling, and the goal is not to suppress negative emotions and gaslight ourselves into being happy or upbeat all the time. I've also incorporated more work around distinguishing between intuition and learned bias so I know which thoughts and feelings to trust.

In *Awakened*, each principle I'll share will be explained in terms of this blend of my own experiences, scientific research, and psychological and sociological findings. The process of my awakening has been deeply personal, and I've been very transparent about it in this book, sharing some of my biggest failures and distorted thought processes.

I haven't overcome every bad habit or healed every old emotional wound, but I'm so much further along now than when I started, and I believe that sharing what I've learned will help those who are on the journey toward their own awakening.

Some of what I share will make sense for where you're at, and I hope you apply those principles to your life. Other things won't resonate, and that's okay, too.

As you question my ideas and beliefs, you'll emerge with a stronger sense of who you are and where you're headed. Wrestle with the ideas in this book, and use any cynicism or disagreement that arises to bring you closer to your truth.

What I want to share with you through *Awakened* is simply a mindset that I have found invaluable as an educator. Your path to developing resilience may be similar to or completely different from mine, but I believe that working toward a renewed way of thinking will make you a more effective teacher. And more importantly, you'll develop habits that lead to a deeper and unshakeable sense of contentment, motivation, and purpose.

Change the way you think about your job

If you've ever tried to explain to someone who's not in education why teaching is so time- and energy- intensive, you've probably noticed it's a hard problem to pinpoint.

A simple, research-based way to understand it is through two ratios that determine how stressful a profession feels to its workers: effort/reward and demand/control.

When there's a high level of effort required to effectively complete the job but there's a disproportionately low reward (e.g. little financial compensation, few opportunities for promotion and recognition, and a low level of respect), the job is often perceived as stressful. There's an imbalance in the effort/reward ratio.

A job is also considered stressful if the demand/control ratio is out of balance. When the work entails excessive, never-ending, high stakes demands, but the employee is allowed very little control or influence over the day-to-day operations, that often leads to chronic stress and burnout.

Unfortunately, working in a K-12 school in the United States tends to be both high effort/low reward *and* high-demand/low control.

Educators are held responsible for factors beyond our reach. We cannot change home environments or compensate for institutional shortcomings and under-resourced communities. We cannot control students' motivation and effort levels, or the way they behave. Usually we can't even control the curriculum, standards, and pacing of our lessons.

The stress we feel comes from this huge disparity between our level of *influence* over these issues and our level of *accountability* for them.

Educators are expected to produce a pre-determined outcome regardless of the lack of support, time, or resources provided. This makes the high effort/low reward ratio even more extreme.

We continually up our efforts even though the reward doesn't increase correspondingly, because what's the alternative in an under-funded system in which both human and physical resources are always scarce? We give of ourselves at the expense of our own well-being in order to strive toward goals that we did not set and are not equipped to meet.

Is it any wonder that teaching has become one of the most emotionally taxing jobs in our society?

People who work in professions with high demand/low control and high effort/low reward ratios tend to burn out quickly. According to a wide body of research, these workers are more likely to have heart and cardiovascular problems, high cholesterol, back pain, injuries, anxiety, depression, and higher incidences of alcohol and prescription drug use.

Some research has found that stress-related illnesses are not present when teachers are provided with adequate resources, such as emotional support, decision-making flexibility, and sufficient teaching materials. Unfortunately, these working environments are the exception.

Chances are, the research backs what you already know from personal experience: teaching is highly stressful in most schools, and the type of stress it involves can have a profoundly negative effect on us.

So what can a teacher do to balance out the demand/control and effort/reward ratios when the entire education system needs to be reimagined? Is it possible to somehow:

- Lessen the demands we feel?
- Increase our perception of control?
- Decrease the mental and emotional energy we expend?
- Enhance our positive, rewarding feelings?

Absolutely. That's exactly what this book will help you do.

Who creates the stress in your life?

How well you deal with stress depends partially on whether you view it as coming from within you or outside of you. That is, do you perceive challenging circumstances as the sole source of stress, or can you recognize how *your response* to challenging circumstances increases or decreases your stress level?

This is not to imply that our feelings are the primary problem: clearly, there are injustices and inadequacies in our systems that need to change. However, we are better equipped to advocate for ourselves and our students when we understand the way our stress response works and when we know how to manage it.

Sometimes stress is described as a physical symptom, such as a headache, high blood pressure, or fatigue, since these signs are easily recognizable. However, when we feel stress in our bodies, it's often due to unseen mental or emotional strain that only later manifests through physical ailments.

With the exception of trauma responses (which we'll delve into shortly), stress generally starts in our *minds*, often without us even realizing it. We think stressed out thoughts, and then we feel stressed out emotions, and our bodies bear the results.

Our thoughts (opinions and ideas) about an event have a huge impact on whether we react calmly or feel anxious and upset. If we view the things that are happening around us in a negative way, a stress reaction will automatically be triggered.

This is the opposite of how most of us understand stress. Often people believe that stress comes from external sources, such as a disrespectful student or an overly demanding administrator. However, your perception of those interactions—the way you think about them—is what determines whether you feel stressed or not.

One teacher might think, *This is intolerable! It should not be happening! I can't handle this and shouldn't have to deal with it!* These thoughts trigger feelings of anger and anxiety which, when left unchecked, can lead to physical symptoms of stress.

Another teacher might think, *This is frustrating, but it's not going to ruin my day. I won't take the situation personally and I'll handle it the best I can.* These thoughts lead to a calmer emotional state and don't trigger a strong stress reaction in the body.

We have the ability to choose different framings of a situation, and move between them if we'd like (perhaps staying in the angry framing for a bit, then selecting a gentler framing that feels better.)

Choosing to define stress as something that *happens to you* steals your power to handle it effectively. When you perceive a cause-effect relationship between life events and your emotional response (e.g. student talks back, therefore I get upset), you begin to believe you can't do anything about the situation.

After all, if you feel stress because of an outside event, then the outside event must change for you to feel better. If you can't change the outside event (like a child's behavior or a school policy), you feel hopeless, frustrated, and overwhelmed.

There are many resources for teachers that address how to manage the external contributors to stress. You can learn how to foster the home-school connection, how to help motivate students, and how to organize and manage your classroom. You can practice self-care, keep your body as healthy as possible, and make sure you're getting proper sleep.

These issues are important, obviously, or I wouldn't have addressed them so thoroughly in my other books, blog, and podcast. However, these outward changes have a limited ability to reduce stress if your thinking process is still distorted.

In a profession and society in which so much is beyond your control, you can take charge of your mindset: the way YOU think and perceive things, and the way YOU choose to respond.

If you want to create meaningful and lasting change in your job satisfaction, the best place to start is with your own thought patterns and attitude. A healthy mindset will fortify you with the mental and emotional strength needed to create systemic change and advocate for better conditions for teaching and learning.

The power of perception: there's no such thing as a "bad" school

My first revelation about the power of one's mindset came in November 2004, right when I started on my new personal development path and shortly after both moving and transferring to a new school in South Florida.

The school was overcrowded, and there had been delays in obtaining portable classrooms, so several teachers were forced to share classrooms. This meant I'd be co-teaching 46 elementary students in a single room.

The teacher I'd be sharing my classroom with—I'll call her Kate— had also just transferred from a work environment she found challenging, and we both really liked our new school.

Kate and I clicked instantly and formed a strong partnership. We were surprised at how amazingly well-behaved and eager to learn our students were despite the chaos of having 46 kids in the room.

But we immediately encountered a small group of teachers who warned us about how terrible the school was. They complained endlessly about how the kids had no self-discipline and the parents didn't care. They proclaimed that no one could possibly teach well in such a poorly-run environment with a difficult student body and overcrowded classrooms.

We were astonished.

How could they possibly think *this* was a bad school? Kate and I constantly reaffirmed to one another that teaching at this particular school was remarkably easy after what we'd experienced elsewhere.

The naysayers wouldn't quit, and after two weeks of listening to them drone on and on everyday at lunch, Kate shared with them what was on her mind in a calm and matter-of-fact way.

"This place is a walk in the park compared to where I'm from. You can't imagine what folks there are facing on a daily basis. If you think this is such a horrible place to teach, you can request a transfer to my old school—I know there's vacancies right now."

The complainers were stunned and out of excuses for once, and the conversation turned to our weekend plans. But the negativity returned again the following week, and Kate and I began eating in our classroom together rather than in the faculty lounge.

That encounter really challenged my thinking about what it meant to enjoy being a teacher. The complainers were facing all the same difficulties my co-teacher and I were (and actually they had it easier, as they had normal class sizes and their own classrooms.) Yet we perceived things so differently it was almost as if we weren't in the same school.

While they grumbled about overcrowding, Kate and I saw it as a blessing in disguise because we got the incredible experience of having a friend/co-teacher by our side every moment of the school day. We believed that we were in a position to make a difference for the students and their families, and were determined to do so. When problems arose, we saw them as the exception, rather than the rule, and recognized how many good things we had going for us in the school.

We had a completely different mindset, and therefore a completely different experience at work.

The complainers left each day more discouraged and depressed than the day before; we left energized and chatting excitedly about the possibilities for the future.

Listening to other teachers bitterly fault-find the most functional school environment I'd ever experienced had made the importance of one's mindset abundantly clear. I began to realize how much a person's outlook affects their stress level every moment of every day.

Your mindset is ultimately the reason why you love teaching or despise it. There is no such thing as a "good school" or "bad teaching position"; workplaces and jobs are not *inherently* good or bad. Your circumstances can certainly make the work harder than it needs to be, but whether you enjoy your work is largely within your own frame of reference.

This understanding was a major awakening for me. I was happy at that point in my career, but I still needed to learn that I had *control* over my mindset and stress level.

I didn't yet realize that my internal state could be completely independent of my external environment.

After all, my happiness at that point came from liking my job. If my circumstances were to change—if we got a new principal, or if I were moved to a different grade level—I knew I would quickly become unhappy again. I recognized that my job satisfaction was temporary: the new school was good, but only in comparison to my old school which had been much more demanding.

Deep down, I was worried. What would happen once I settled in? Would I revert back to my old patterns?

Kate was the total opposite. She's one of those "nothing gets me down, look on the bright side" people by nature. Kate was content even when she was teaching in the most challenging environments, and simply brought her positive attitude everywhere she went. I marveled at how good natured she was, but didn't think I could ever possess such happy-go-lucky qualities.

Since we were spending 40 hours a week in the same room together, I watched Kate very carefully and began to consciously model my outlook after hers.

I noticed that when something frustrating would happen and I'd want to gripe about it, Kate would brush off the incident and refocus our discussion on something productive.

She refused to gossip and never wasted any energy tearing others down behind their backs.

When I worried that a problem would escalate and become insurmountable, Kate would ground the conversation with a more realistic perspective and draw attention to the way I'd catastrophized things.

During the school day, I observed Kate's reactions and practiced taking her light-hearted, humorous approach to setbacks. I surrounded myself with other encouraging teachers and limited the amount of time I spent with the ones who were always unhappy.

Then in the evenings, I'd immerse myself in all sorts of books and other media that helped me learn to have a productive, healthy mindset no matter what was happening around me. Throughout that school year, I carefully filtered the friends and influences in my life so that I was surrounded with people and ideas that uplifted and encouraged me. I practiced thinking constructive thoughts and rooted out the thought patterns that were making me unhappy.

And to my utter amazement, I found as the weeks passed that this new mindset was becoming a *habit*. My default emotion was no longer worry or depression; it was contentment, even when things weren't ideal.

I started to realize that Kate and I were responding to classroom problems in the exact same way without her having to 'talk me down' first. I didn't have to consciously *try* to frame things in the positive anymore or struggle to enjoy daily life—my new mindset had become like second nature.

The research behind the power of thought work

Our temperaments are for the most part inherent traits that we exhibit from a young age. Some people are naturally happier and upbeat; some are more melancholy by nature.

But, it IS possible to change your outlook and the way you perceive the world.

If you've ever thought, "I am the way I am—I can't change the way I think or feel," please know that you absolutely CAN change your thoughts, emotions, behaviors, and reaction to stress if you want to.

Not only is my life the evidence…it's been scientifically proven for decades, in study after study.

Researchers in the field of positive psychology have found that even the most die-hard pessimistic thinkers can become optimists. It's called *learned optimism,* and it's simply a matter of choosing to change how you think.

You've probably heard of learned helplessness; this is the exact opposite. Martin Seligman is the world-renowned psychologist who coined both terms in the late 1960s and dedicated his life to the study of them.

Seligman found that both pessimistic and optimistic world views are learned (not inborn), and can therefore be *unlearned.* He teaches a set of mental frameworks you can build to protect yourself from potentially destructive influences such as a stressful workplace.

His research in positive psychology has shown that anyone can actively change thought patterns which reinforce the idea that stressful situations will never change, that you're the victim or cause of them, or that your job is keeping you from being happy.

Seligman demonstrated how you can learn to change the way you think—and thereby the way you experience and enjoy life—through a specific process of re-attributing thoughts and healthy habits.

The positive psychology movement that Seligman pioneered can be understood as the scientific study of what helps humans flourish and live their best lives. It focuses on promoting strengths and centers optimal functioning, rather than uncovering or "fixing" flaws.

However, his techniques are just one of many effective approaches. There is an entire field aligned with positive psychology known as cognitive-behavioral therapy (or CBT, pioneered in the 1960's by Aaron T. Beck) that is dedicated to helping people overcome problems by changing their thinking, emotional response, and behaviors.

Dr. Albert Ellis, who worked closely with Beck, furthered our understanding of the field with his premise that it's not circumstances in life that upset us, but our *beliefs* (thoughts and perceptions) about those circumstances that cause feelings of anxiety, anger, depression, and so on.

CBT teaches people how to change irrational beliefs (such as, "I must be treated fairly all the time in life and get what I want or I'll be miserable") into more rational ones ("There is no reason to believe I will always be treated fairly or get everything I want; I may be disappointed or uncomfortable, but setbacks won't be unbearable.")

A newer form of CBT was developed by Steven Hayes in the 1980s and grew to prominence in the early 2000s. It's called Dialectical Behavior Therapy. DBT addresses destructive thoughts and behaviors while also incorporating emotional regulation and mindfulness strategies. It's called "dialectical" because it brings together the opposite approaches of acceptance and change, which proponents say produces better results than either strategy alone.

During the same time period, Dr. Marsha Linehan was developing Acceptance and Commitment Therapy (ACT). Her approach uses acceptance and mindfulness strategies combined with behavior change strategies to increase psychological flexibility. The goal is help people be open to unpleasant feelings so we don't avoid or overreact to them.

DBT---and even more so, ACT---have grown in popularity over the last few years among people for whom CBT has not been comprehensive enough. This is particularly true for people managing mental illness or trauma, and for those facing stressors that arise from inequities and institutional failures.

To put it bluntly, thinking accurate thoughts about societal, economic, political, or ecological collapse can be extremely distressing. Combining rational thoughts with a practice of acceptance and committing to change can be far more empowering.

Today, CBT, DBT, and ACT are three of the most widely-practiced therapies in the world. These approaches (along with the broader positive psychology movement) have been a huge influence on the suggestions in this book.

Perhaps you're not a fan of psychology and wouldn't dream of reading a self-help book. That's okay—countless people have changed their mindset through both formal and informal self-development work. My own approach was intuitive, rather than based on a prescribed set of steps or practices. Clearly, there are many effective approaches to developing a new mindset for teaching and for life.

The most important thing to remember is that you cannot avoid all sources of stress or lessen all the demands of your job, but you CAN alter your mindset and behavior—and that can make all the difference.

The process of actively seeing a situation in a different light (called *reframing* by researcher Virginia Satir) allows us to let go of thoughts that are limiting and open ourselves up to new possibilities.

Learning to reframe is not the sole solution, and positive psychology practices focused on helping you flourish won't solve everything. But, they *are* a set of highly impactful tools that can create change which permeates every aspect of your work and life.

Create change by letting go instead of trying harder

Though I'll teach you many tools for changing your thinking, I want to be clear that this process does NOT need to involve intense effort, deep study, or highly focused efforts to "be a better person."

In fact, most of us have overcomplicated our lives with our thinking. The most important work is often in letting go of what's not serving us well, in order to reveal the more content, peaceful person at our core.

Think back to some moments you are most proud of as a teacher. They were most likely times when you were fully present as your most essential self. Those were times when you were authentically YOU.

During those moments, you were vulnerable, took risks, and totally immersed yourself in caring for and supporting your students.

That is your essential self.

It's unburdened by to-do lists, standards, and outside expectations. It's free from unhelpful stories about what is and isn't possible. It's you in your most authentic state: present, loving, and filled with purpose.

You don't have to try to be anything that you are not. And that includes the positive ways of being that you wish you embodied. You can let go of the striving.

Focus instead on just being your true, whole, healed, essential self, letting go of any thoughts, beliefs, and actions that don't serve the highest good. At your core, you are loving, patient, kind, and compassionate. You are full of life and energy and purpose.

All the traits that are counter to that are simply baggage and coping mechanisms you've picked up along the way in your journey through life in a very challenging world. They're reactions you've developed as a result of fear, emotional wounds, defensiveness, prejudice, biases, outside expectations, and so on.

You've accumulated triggers — things that set you off so you don't respond in the way you wish you could. You've accumulated habits and patterns that aren't serving you well. You're responding from a place of pain or as a result of trauma and suffering.

That's all part of the journey of being human. But those things aren't really you. At your core, you have a beautiful spirit or soul or essential self, however you choose to see it.

So you don't have to constantly work hard to become a better teacher (or partner, or parent). You're not *becoming* anything.

You're simply releasing all the habits and patterns that aren't really you. Being yourself — your true essential self — is always enough. It's always exactly what's needed at any given moment.

So, instead of getting down on yourself when you recognize unhealthy thoughts, think about what you need to release. Think about what is holding you back from doing what you want and need to do.

For example, when you find yourself yelling at a student, remember that your natural state — the real you — is calm, patient, and loving. What happened to pull you out of that state?

Were you replaying all the times in the past when that student pushed your buttons, or projecting ahead to the future and thinking about how you couldn't possibly keep dealing with that behavior until June?

Were you caught off guard — trying to focus on something else in the moment, and unprepared to handle the situation with the full presence and calmness that was needed?

Release yourself from judgment, and simply observe. Notice what pulled you out of your natural state and into a reactive behavior or habit or pattern that you don't like. Awareness is the goal.

Often the reason why we don't follow through with what we wish we could do — be it eating healthy, exercising, being patient with others, or getting work done instead of procrastinating — is because we're weighed down with a bunch of stuff that we need to let go of.

We've accumulated habits in the evenings that waste time and keep us from getting a good night's sleep. We've fallen into patterns of buying junk food and not nourishing our bodies properly. We've defaulted into taking care of everyone else's needs and never noticing what our bodies, hearts, and minds are crying out for us to do.

We're not really keyed into our senses and the things that bring us joy. When you return to those things — when you take a moment to breathe, or meditate, or stare out the window, or take a hot bath, or light a candle and watch the flame flicker, or savor a meal with someone you care about — those things allow us to return to our essential selves. These activities feed our souls. They remind us of who we are, and what really matters. They bring us back to the present.

What we need is less about *becoming someone* or *doing something*, and more about loving who we are and accepting ourselves. Then we can release ourselves from expectations, habits, and patterns that aren't serving us well.

This is simply a moment-by-moment choice. When you feel things spinning out of control, take that moment to re-center yourself. Observe what's happening, and tune into what you need in that moment: a quick break, a drink of water, switching to another task, etc. Pay attention to your own needs instead of just trying to push through.

When you do that, you're able to return to your essential self more quickly. That's the natural state you want to spend as much time in as possible, where you are able to respond to the world around you from a proactive rather than reactive space.

The beautiful thing about learning to treat yourself with this much compassion and kindness is that it helps you treat others that way, too. As you practice releasing yourself from judgment, you can do the same for people around you.

Take your students, for example. At the core, they have beautiful souls and kind hearts. What is happening to pull them out of that state?

How can you meet them with understanding so that they, too, can become more mindful of their habits and triggers and patterns?

Releasing yourself, your students, your colleagues, your family members, your partner — anyone in your life — from judgment is an ongoing practice but it will change your life.

It's definitely changed mine, starting with a small mindset shift that rippled out into every aspect of my being. It feels very different when you see yourself as inherently flawed and in need of constant fixing and improvement, and instead, choose to see your essential self as wonderful and trustworthy.

Growing as a person then becomes an act of returning to yourself and embracing who you really are, instead of trying to constantly change or improve yourself.

Your very existence, your presence in the classroom, has value. And the more that you show up with an open heart and mind, free from limiting beliefs about yourself, your students, and your school, the more your essential self will shine through.

2

You are not your thoughts

Have you ever noticed how many unwanted thoughts pop into your head on a daily basis?

For example, consider how many times you've replayed an unpleasant conversation in your mind, mulling over all the things you could have said and done differently, even if the interaction happened long ago.

This was certainly true for me. If the school secretary was a bit snippy with me one time, that's the memory that would resurface in my mind periodically for weeks or even months, no matter how nice she had been in every other encounter.

My mind didn't seem to replay the countless positive conversations, but any conflicts in my life (no matter how minor) would come up out of nowhere. I'd be watching TV or grading papers and suddenly remember a problem.

I also noticed my mind would wander to judgmental rants: I'd make a mental list of why a particular parent was unfit or how a certain student was beyond help: *See, this is exactly why Anthony isn't reading on grade level—he's talking while I'm teaching, he hasn't turned in his classwork in days, he was late seven times this month, and his parents took him out of school for a week to go on vacation. Ridiculous!*

Subconsciously, my mind would continue to collect more data that reinforced what I already believed. The confirmation bias created a signal to my brain each time: *Aha! Another piece of evidence to add to our running tally of Everything That's Wrong with Anthony.*

Often, I'd use those mental rants to formulate predictions about what would happen next—I'd anticipate problems and jump to conclusions in my haste to assume the worst. *I bet he won't bring his homework tomorrow, either. This kid is going nowhere in life. It's so sad. I'm completely wasting my time. Why bother trying with him anymore?*

I knew I couldn't act on those thoughts or let them show, and I fooled myself into thinking that the kids weren't perceptive enough to pick up on my real feelings.

My goal was to treat all students equitably and with compassion, but my thought system made that task impossibly exhausting. I had to put on an act with my students, and behave in a way that was out of alignment with what I was thinking and feeling.

I had a challenging situation with this student, no doubt, but the story I was telling myself about it drained my energy far more than necessary. Obviously this was unfair to Anthony, but what I didn't realize at the time was how unfair I was being to myself.

As humans, we are happiest when our beliefs and behaviors are healthy and in alignment. But when the things we're thinking are toxic and harmful to our relationships, we wind up stuffing them deep inside, where they eventually poison our own wellbeing.

Maybe my confessions so far have made me sound like a bad person, but these kinds of struggles are pretty common. Most people's minds are full of random thoughts, some of which are mean and unfair. All kinds of ideas can pop into our heads totally unbidden.

And, our brains are pattern-seeking. This inclination allows us to process and filter information with less effort, which is good, but it also means we can easily get stuck in thought patterns that are destructive and not even realize what's happening.

Our brains often function like a treadmill that powers up to full speed the moment we wake up. Our minds force us to race along and process every thought that occurs to us, whether we want to keep up or not. And then when night falls, our brains refuse to shut down and we lie awake ruminating some more.

Rarely are we fully present in our experiences because our brains are busy thinking about what already happened and trying to predict and control what will happen next. Many of these thoughts are unnecessary and ultimately unproductive.

Intrusive, unwanted thoughts come in many forms and are deeply shaped by our past experiences. I find myself often tending toward cynical, complaining, anxious, pensive, judgmental, and depressed thought patterns. Maybe your struggle is with thoughts of guilt, shame, self-doubt, inferiority, regret, anger, bitterness, or fear.

However, it doesn't matter what type of thoughts are bringing you down.

It doesn't matter what caused the thoughts.

It doesn't really even matter whether they're true or not.

What matters is that the thoughts are counter-productive: they weaken rather than strengthen, and you can choose to shift your focus to the thoughts that strengthen you.

For years, it never occurred to me that I could select which ideas to dwell on and which to let go. I assumed that if I forced myself to stop thinking about something, it would be equivalent to repressing my thoughts—some unhealthy process that would lead to a mental breakdown or subconscious outburst. I worried that if I didn't fully explore those negative thoughts and feelings, they would fester and worsen.

After much practice in re-training my mind, I realized this simply wasn't true. Ruminating endlessly on all the things that were "wrong" with me only made those issues seem more overwhelming and impossible to solve.

With time, I learned that there was usually no reason to replay a negative event from the past or worry about the future. I discovered that I wasn't obligated to dwell on every fleeting idea that passed through my brain.

And, I learned that I could let an idea go; notice that it popped into my head, and choose to let it pass without it affecting my state of mind or emotions.

Rather than identifying with our thoughts—seeing them as inherently true and valid, simply because they popped into our minds—we can choose to observe our thoughts from an outside perspective:

Look at me, getting all worked up about this little issue again. So interesting how this particular trigger results in judgmental thoughts about my students. I can observe that those thoughts passed through my mind, but they're not "my" thoughts. I don't own them, I didn't intentionally create them, and other people have thought them before. They're not mine, and they're not ME. They're just thoughts, and I don't have to give them any further attention. I can choose a different thought to focus on anytime I want.

How thoughts take root in our minds

The process of choosing your thoughts may seem not only impossible to you, but strange and perhaps even unnecessary. Why is it so important to choose your thoughts, especially if you're not acting on them or sharing them with someone else? What's so dangerous about just *thinking* something?

Each thought in your mind is like a seed that grows into a mindset (a way of thinking or an attitude.) Your mindset influences your feelings and emotions, then manifests through your actions, and your actions become behavioral patterns. Therefore, the way that you experience life is directly related to the thoughts you allow to take root in your brain.

Unwanted, counter-productive thoughts stay planted in your mind. You may not realize it because they can take awhile to bloom if you don't water and fertilize them regularly with more negativity.

But, whatever you sow, you will eventually reap. Those negative seeds stay planted there for hours, days, weeks, even years…but eventually, unless you actively weed them out, the seeds will bloom.

Let's say this thought pops into your head when a child is daydreaming: *This student is completely unmotivated. She never pays attention when I teach.*

Although this thought is understandable, it's quite negative and counterproductive because it unfairly over-generalizes the child's behavior (NEVER pays attention?) and makes an impossible judgment about her internal state (totally unmotivated and doesn't want to do anything, at all, ever?)

If you allow that story to stay in your mind all morning by repeatedly thinking about it, it becomes rooted there and creates corresponding emotions like discouragement and frustration.

Then later that afternoon when someone asks you how that student is doing, the negative seed you planted will bloom—it will be the first thing you think of—and you'll repeat your thoughts about what happened: "She's not doing well, actually. She never pays attention."

Even if the topic (and therefore your conscious thought) doesn't appear to surface, that root of negativity will still stay in your mind and grow.

Three days later when the child yawns during one of your lessons, your pattern-seeking brain will remind you: *See, I knew it! She's unmotivated. She doesn't pay attention.*

If you're not alert, you'll accept that voice as a true observation of what's happening and act on it. But if you're perceptive and aware, you'll realize that the negative refrain is growth from the negative seed you sowed long ago.

Confirmation bias—the brain's tendency to accept evidence that backs up what you already believe and disregard evidence that contradicts your beliefs— will convince you that your perception *must* be true.

If you don't filter out those inaccurate perceptions, you'll soon find yourself on a downward emotional spiral. Your critical thoughts will become automatic and you'll no longer be aware that you're thinking them.

They'll become rooted in your unconscious thought system, which is self-validating. This means that your mind reinforces those beliefs every time it perceives more evidence for them: *Oh, she's playing with her phone—typical! Her attention span is zero.* Your brain filters out the fact that the student wasn't playing with her phone for the entire first half hour of the lesson; your thought system only focuses on the events that reinforce what you already believe.

This is how constant frustration and feelings of stress begin. When another student starts digging through his backpack during your lesson, that same thought about distraction and laziness will return. You'll find yourself whining in the teacher's lounge about how your entire class is unmotivated and doesn't care about their education. Someone else will chime in with their own stories and solidify what your mind now sees as an indisputable fact about reality.

Your new attitude will make you feel disheartened and affect the way you behave toward your class, until one exhausting day when you're pulling your hair out and asking yourself, *When did I become so bitter and jaded??*

It all started with unchecked negative thoughts and inaccurate conclusions.

Perhaps that sounds dramatic or over-simplified, but I know for certain that many of my moments of burnout were directly correlated to the way I chose to think about my work. I let negative thoughts cloud my mind so much that I could no longer see the good things or enjoy my job.

Some esoteric philosophers teach that thoughts and feelings are objectively neither good nor bad, so therefore we should not attach judgment to them and just allow them to be. (We'll dig deeper into non-attachment and non-judgment in later chapters, as I've found them incredibly useful principles.)

However, in this specific context, I like the Cognitive Behavioral Therapy (CBT) tools which can help us judge thoughts and beliefs according to whether they are rational and productive or irrational and counter-productive. In this approach, you simply identify whether the way you are thinking and feeling is contributing to your overall wellbeing and determine your response accordingly.

Here's how that works in the previous example about believing a student is unmotivated. If we examine that thought objectively, we can tell it's irrational (because it applies a broad label as a result of over-generalizing) and also counter-productive (because it does not facilitate positive teacher-student interactions.)

The thought that "This student doesn't care about their education" creates feelings that don't contribute to your wellbeing, and instead stirs up discouragement and frustration.

Therefore for our purposes here, that thought would be considered distorted. It's an inaccurate perception and does not contribute to positive, healthy functioning.

Fortunately, thoughts only *hold* power if you give them attention and attach importance. You are not doomed to experience sadness even if negative thoughts enter your mind all day long. Feelings of irritation do not have to result in rage. A sense of being overwhelmed doesn't have to develop into helplessness, exhaustion, and despair. You can choose your mindset by focusing only on the thoughts that are wanted.

In principle, it's just that simple: determine the way you want to think, and disregard any thoughts that don't align with your choice.

If you choose to believe that teaching is an important calling and you are making a difference in the lives of children, disregard any thought that insists otherwise. Dismiss thoughts like, *I'm totally disorganized, I'm so bad at teaching math,* and *I can't get through to these kids.* Your thoughts are not immutable truth. They are simply thoughts.

Of course, reality can be much more complicated, and for most of us to apply this principle, a great deal of practice in retraining our brains is required. That's to be expected—we've established mental habits over a period of many years, and now they have to be unlearned. You'll find strategies for letting go of unwanted thoughts and choosing constructive thoughts all throughout this book, beginning with four basic all-purpose strategies explained in the next chapter.

But before we get to practical techniques that work, let's examine some natural human reactions that *don't* work at all.

How NOT to combat unwanted thoughts

1) Don't assume your thoughts are all accurate and objective.

Just because a thought popped into your mind, doesn't mean it's true. You wouldn't accept without question every statement other people make to you, and it's important to use that same level of discernment with your own thoughts.

Cognitive biases (systematic patterns of irrationality) color the way we see the world. We each have our own construction of reality, or personal viewpoint, and we don't see things objectively *even when it feels that way.*

All of us make inaccurate judgments and illogical interpretations. Each of us is living in our own subjective reality, in which our worldview makes total sense to us but almost certainly contains cognitive bias.

For example, I've mentioned confirmation bias (the tendency to search for, interpret, and recall information in a way that supports our existing beliefs).

You'll also notice recency bias creeping in: events that happened recently weigh more heavily in our minds, and we often remember the last thing we heard or saw more than the first thing.

We also tend toward negativity biases, which predispose us to focus on the bad. This is a survival strategy, since for early humans, it would have been difficult to stay alive if our brains weren't always attuned to possible threats.

Confirmation bias, recency bias, and negativity bias may play out by creating unpleasant associations that aren't really true. You may dread checking your email, for example, if you've recently had a negative interaction. That unsettled feeling is because your brain is preparing you for bad news or conflict: you're unconsciously recalling previous times when things didn't go well and anticipating more problems.

From an objective standpoint, the majority of times when you check your email, you won't see anything upsetting. But, the times when you *have* read something you don't like stand out more in your mind. This causes you to believe that something bad is likely to be there even though the chances are smaller.

Throughout this book, we'll delve more deeply into how to root out different types of bias and understand the stories we're telling ourselves within our own separately created realities.

But for now: start with the understanding that your thoughts are not all objectively true and need to be evaluated.

2) Don't ruminate endlessly on unwanted thoughts or try to work through them solely with logic.

As a young teacher, I often tried to reason my way through dysfunctional thinking: *Why is this bothering me? What made me think that? Why do I feel this way? What is wrong with me?*

I assumed that if I mulled over a thought or feeling in my head for long enough (or talked to enough people, or analyzed myself with enough books by experts), I'd figure out why I thought the way I did and fix it.

This led to being overly analytical and self-occupied. My issues became all-consuming and loomed even greater in my head. "Fixing" my mental habits became one more exhausting thing I had to deal with.

The flaw in trying to understand your thoughts is that thinking is not always logical. There is no rational explanation for all the things that pop into our minds.

Your mindset has been influenced by everything from childhood events to the random T.V. show you watched for half an hour last summer. And, past traumas and upsetting experiences can play out in baffling ways. Trying to figure out why you are the way you are can be a frustrating pursuit, because our thoughts and reactions aren't necessarily rooted in a logical system.

Through the process of paying attention to my thoughts and countering irrational ideas, there were many light bulb moments in which I realized the root cause of an issue. But, understanding what caused the thought was a side effect, not the end goal.

So, don't focus too much of your energy on trying to understand WHY. You are not your thoughts; you are the observer of your thoughts. If you don't like a thought that pops into your head, you don't have to identify with it, analyze it, and give it any further attention.

3) Don't rationalize that negative thoughts are okay as long as you're not talking about or acting on them.

This misconception is extremely pervasive in our culture—it's socially acceptable to silently harbor judgmental, petty, rude sentiments as long as you don't express them. Since childhood, we've been taught adages like, "If you don't have anything nice to say, don't say anything at all" and "Some things you should just think in your head and not share out loud."

Yes, these principles prevent others from being hurt. But most of us were never told that repeating negativity *in our own minds* can cause great damage. Even if you don't act on your unwanted thoughts, they will unavoidably influence the way you think and behave down the line.

There have been many times when I used an exasperated tone with someone or responded harshly toward them for seemingly no reason, only to recall later that I had allowed myself to complain in my mind at some point.

For example, I might think, *Our science teacher Mr. Smith is always wanting me to do something for him. When was the last time he did something to make MY job easier? I've done this, that, and the other for his classes…why doesn't he pull his weight?*

The next time we saw each other and Mr. Smith asked me to stop by his room after school, I'd feel irritation rising up inside me.

Unwanted thoughts like, *Here we go again! He always wants something from me!* would surface in my mind, and I'd have to bite back my nasty tone. I had allowed some bitterness to build up through replaying negative thoughts and sure enough, that caused me to speak and behave in ways that I hadn't intended.

Negative thoughts are like seeds of poison that choke out and kill off everything inside you that's kind and loving, even if you never say a word to anyone about them. A person's thoughts and mindset become obvious through their behavior.

And if we're honest, most of us DO share our negative thoughts aloud. We just fool ourselves into thinking we're entitled to certain exceptions. We figure we can grumble with a best friend or partner and it "doesn't count" as gossip or complaining as long as no one else knows. Through this rationalization, we unconsciously spread the poison of negativity to the people closest to us and allow it to grow and fester.

So, don't create excuses for permitting unwanted thoughts to remain in your mind. Allowing exceptions by telling yourself, "I need to vent" won't undo the destruction caused by extensive negative reflection. By the time you've replayed the problem in your mind a hundred times and desperately need to unload all your anxiety or anger onto someone else, the damage is already done!

The solution is to focus your attention on not letting the dysfunctional thoughts repeat in your mind. If you stop *creating* feelings of frustration through pervasive negative thoughts, there will be nothing to vent about!

Remember, once you've validated unwanted thoughts by ruminating on and voicing them, you've already planted the seed for something you don't want to bloom.

Sometimes it takes only a few minutes of worrying to devolve into full-blown anxiety, and a few minutes of complaining to devolve into feelings of depression. Don't take that risk. You will pay the price in one form or another eventually. Peter McWilliams sums the sentiment up perfectly: "You can't afford the luxury of a negative thought."

4) Don't be too hard on yourself for falling into negative or distorted thought patterns.

Obviously, you won't be able to avoid ALL negative or irrational thoughts completely and permanently. No one can be totally rational 100% of the time. Be prepared to slip into old habits on occasion—and quite often in the beginning. It will happen multiple times per day or even hour.

Accepting that it WILL happen keeps you from being caught off-guard. It prevents you from getting sucked into more negative thoughts like, *I can't believe I did that again, I'm never going to get my thinking straightened out, I just can't do this.*

Your slip-ups do not prove that you're unable to change. They only prove that you need to keep practicing your new mental habits until they're automatic.

The "no excuses" rule regarding negative thoughts simply means that you shouldn't create exceptions and justify your slip-ups. It doesn't mean you should upset yourself when you fall short.

When you allow unwanted thoughts to stay in your mind, consciously acknowledge that's what happened, and move on: *Whoops, that was definitely an example of the distorted thinking I used to allow all the time in my head. This time, I realized what I did afterward. That's progress. With more practice, I know I'll be able to catch those unwanted thoughts earlier.*

Allowing your mind to process and contemplate every random thought that pops into your head is a habit you created over many years. Don't get discouraged when your mind reverts back to that. Be forgiving of yourself, and vigilantly aware of what's happening *right now* in your mind. You'll start to see improvement very quickly.

5) Don't avoid medication, therapy, and counseling if needed.

Though clinical depression and anxiety are beyond the scope of this book, I want to be clear that *you don't have to address mental health on your own.*

I went to a number of counselors and psychologists in my teens and twenties. I was also medicated for bipolar disorder, primarily regulating my dopamine levels by taking a small "cocktail" of drugs.

In my early thirties, I slowly went off the medications (under the supervision of my doctor) and reached a point where I could deal with low-level, short periods of depression and hypomania primarily through allowing myself to experience these cycles, and keeping them in check with mindset work and healthy daily habits.

But in the years that followed, I began noticing that irrational anxious thoughts were creeping into my mind more often, and to an extent that I couldn't manage on my own.

I remember one day when I hadn't seen our cat around the house in a couple of hours, and my first thought was: *She escaped from the house despite all the windows and doors being locked, and got hit by a car!* Even though I knew this was an incredibly unlikely scenario, I felt compelled to run to the window to see if she was lying in the street.

Even though my mind didn't work like this all the time, these kind of irrational thoughts were relentless during the start of the pandemic, which was creating daily triggers around many of my worst fears. I worried constantly about everything, and wanted to just lay in bed and "doom scroll" through Twitter to validate my anxieties. I felt the need to overthink and over-plan everything, and it was exhausting.

I told a psychiatrist about this and was prescribed a serotonin-enhancing medication. To my surprise, the first drug was the right one, and I felt a difference within 48 hours. Sertraline primarily prevents anxiety but also keeps my depressive episodes from becoming too severe (lasting a few hours or at most, a day or two.) The serotonin boost keeps me from falling into pits of sadness or just not caring about anything, and also makes me feel like I can go with the flow rather than needing to control or plan for every possible outcome.

For me, anti-anxiety medication goes hand-in-hand with thought work. When I was *only* medicating and not addressing my thought patterns, I often fell into cycles of anxiety and depression. Later, when I was *only* addressing my thought patterns and not medicating, it took Herculean efforts to stay in a healthy mental state.

When I went back on medication, I found that choosing healthy mental habits became infinitely easier, because my body chemistry was no longer working against me. Right now, I feel at my best when I have the support of a serotonin-enhancing medication *and* am actively interrogating my thoughts and beliefs to choose ones that are healthy for me.

My needs—and yours—in the area of mental health will likely change over time as we age and our hormone levels shift. We'll also experience different life circumstances and stressors which can impact whether we benefit from medication and what type(s) are needed.

None of us need to overcome every trauma, negative thought pattern, and bout of anxiety or depression through our own sheer willpower. There are so many tools available that can make changing our mindset and staying mentally balanced less difficult.

The way I see it, life is already hard enough—there's no prize for tackling everything completely on your own. If therapy or medication can help you live life on an easier setting, you deserve to take advantage of those resources. Both have been a complete game-changer for me.

Four strategies for thinking on purpose

If an idea is something that you recognize as negative, irrational, or counter-productive, you can choose not to allow it to take hold in your mind. You can choose to think about something life-affirming, positive, and productive.

So how exactly do you take control of your thoughts? Before we go deeper into recognizing cognitive distortions, I want to introduce 4 strategies for thinking on purpose.

This way, you'll know upfront what to do whenever you recognize a cognitive bias or unhealthy pattern in yourself. As you read the rest of the book, you'll already have these 4 strategies in mind so you can choose which one (or combination of them) to counter anything problematic that you uncover in your thinking.

You can refer to these 4 techniques by any name you want, but I call them *dismiss, distract, reject,* and *replace.* These are foundational strategies that work for every cognitive distortion and bias we'll discuss, so let's take an in-depth look at each one.

Dismiss

This is gentlest, most self-compassionate approach for unwanted thoughts. When you find yourself slipping into distorted thinking, you can simply acknowledge that it's happening without attaching any importance to the thought.

So, if you notice a judgmental, critical, or unproductive thought, think to yourself, *That thought is not a part of me. That thought has no importance. I'm letting that pass.*

You're not analyzing where it came from or why you feel like you do; you're dismissing the thought as irrelevant to your decision about the type of mindset you want.

Thoughts sometimes seem so pressing and all-consuming that you can't imagine NOT thinking them. However, thoughts have no significance in and of themselves. They only have power and importance when you grant it by giving them attention.

I really hate this job and wish I could quit is no more important than *Maybe I should move my desk to the other side of the room.*

Neither thought is necessarily true, and neither is necessarily worth giving your attention to. Although the idea of wanting to quit seems all-encompassing and like it couldn't possibly be ignored, it's simply something that entered your mind. You can choose not to validate it with your attention.

Dismissing thoughts isn't totally counter-intuitive; we have some practice in this process since most of us don't take our dreams literally. When you wake up, the dream seems very real, but if you feel an emotion tied to your dream (anger, panic, etc.), you know those feelings aren't justified. You tell yourself, *It was only a dream.* You dismiss the thoughts your brain created while you were asleep, or take them with a grain of salt knowing that only part of the dream-thoughts are valuable in reality.

You can do the same thing with ideas that pop unbidden into your mind when you're awake: *It was only a thought. It's not necessarily reality.*

When you first start to take control of your thinking, you'll find that dismissed thoughts will resurface. This is very normal in the beginning, because anything you give attention to will return to your mind later.

When you choose to ruminate on a thought, you're sending a message to your brain that the thought is something of importance and therefore should be recalled. Your brain will simply do its job and bring it to your remembrance later.

Each time you dismiss a thought, you're re-training your brain. You're telling it, *This thought is not important. It's not worth going back to.* With time, any idea along that line of thought will be forgotten and won't be brought back up.

Dismissing works well when a thought is "not like you." When something pops into your mind and you wonder, *Where the heck did THAT come from? Why am I thinking that?*, you can just dismiss it. It's not a part of you, so don't assign it importance.

You can also use this strategy when you know you're in a low mood, and then choose to come back to your thoughts later when you've cleared your head. You can choose to think, *I'm not in a good mental state for dealing with this now. I'm going to dismiss these thoughts for the moment and I'll think about the subject again when the mood passes.*

The "dismiss" strategy for unwanted thoughts is my favorite, because it creates distance between myself and what I'm thinking. It's the path of least resistance: you don't have to counter it in any way, just notice and let it go.

Distract

Dismiss and distract often work hand in hand because after dismissing a thought, the mind looks immediately for some other topic or idea to cling to. Therefore, distracting yourself from unwanted thoughts can keep you from returning to them. It's also a great mental response when you're trying to accomplish a task or engage in conversation and your mind wanders to something unrelated and unproductive.

How do you distract? One of the best ways is to turn your attention to whatever you're doing and completely focus on what's happening in the present moment.

Think to yourself, *I'm going to be present and enjoy what's happening right now.* Focus completely on what you're experiencing in your senses. Don't compare it to what you expected or wanted, or critique the situation in any way. Experience the moment just as it is.

Body scans, meditation, and deep breathing are just a few ways to distract yourself away from an unwanted thought pattern and ground yourself in your body.

If your mind is racing, focus on each breath: in for 3 seconds, hold for 3 seconds, out for 3 seconds, hold for 3 seconds. Repeating this breathing pattern can help you return to a calmer state of mind in less than a minute.

You can also distract yourself by changing activities. There are lots of healthy options: going for a walk while talking on the phone to a friend often works for me.

I also like yoga since it requires my brain to focus on holding the asanas (poses.) Sports, dancing, and other physical movement can help you get out of your head and back into your body. Pick something simple and enjoyable for you.

Reject

Reject is a good strategy to use when dismiss and distract aren't effective in keeping the thought away. I like using it for seriously harmful thoughts, and for old patterns that keep playing out.

When I feel triggered or recognize a thought that's tied to pain or insecurities, I practice rejecting that thought and shutting it down immediately. The process is usually like a lecture from the healthy part of my mind to the part of me that wants to allow nonsense to gather in my head:

Oh no, we are NOT going THERE again. That was an unnecessary and totally unproductive train of thought and I'm not going to follow it. If you keep that up, Angela, you're going to be moping around and complaining all day. Let's choose to have a good time with the kids instead. I want to think about this next activity and what needs to be done to make it the best one possible.

When I notice myself going back down familiar mental roads that don't lead anywhere productive, the "reject" strategy allows me to remind myself, *The last time you gave into these kinds of thoughts, they nearly sent you into a depression and your energy was low for days. Every time you let yourself get worked up about this, it ends badly. You deserve so much better. Don't you want to be happy this evening? Let's just relax a bit instead of thinking about upsetting stuff.*

The tone of the "reject" thought process can be no-nonsense and matter-of-fact, or gentle and empathetic. You might phrase things the way you'd talk to a friend who's spiraling a bit. You could also think of what you'd like a friend to say to *you* when a pep talk or bit of tough love is needed, and say those words to yourself.

Note that rejecting a thought is different from suppressing it. Telling yourself, *Don't think about this* is an attempt at suppression. It doesn't work. It's like the old saying about the purple elephant—as soon as you tell yourself not to imagine one, it's the only thing you can see in your mind.

When your mind repeats, *Don't think about that parent who criticized you,* you're naturally reminded of the incident. You're reinforcing the idea that it was important enough to be remembered and recalled later. As long as you're paying attention to a thought, you're giving it power and importance.

Instead of trying not to think about insidious unwanted thoughts, you can confront them head on and mentally label them as counter-productive, weakening, or unwanted:

This thinking does not help me become the best teacher I can be. It tears me down and makes me feel bad about myself. I refuse to indulge in those types of thoughts.

It can also be helpful to remember that most of the thoughts we need to reject aren't even true; they're exaggerated. We start to feel that bad things are worse than they are and worry that their impact will remain forever.

So, you can tell yourself: *Right now my mind is repeating the refrain that I'm hopeless and incompetent. That's a lie and I reject those thoughts. Even though I don't feel like it right now, I know that I have the ability to be successful and I will succeed. The incident that made me feel incompetent is actually just one thing that happened in my life and not indicative of all my capabilities across all time. That's the truth I am choosing to set my mind on.*

The "reject" strategy can be seen as the opposite of the "dismiss" strategy. In some instances, you can simply let thoughts pass through your mind without judgment (dismiss.) In other instances where the same unwanted thoughts keep returning, you can consciously reject those thoughts through your self-talk and change what you're thinking about.

Replace

This final strategy for taking control of your thoughts involves choosing what you DO what to think about. It's pretty simple, because positive thoughts take root in your mind in the same way that negative ones do.

Each time you think, *I love teaching this unit; My kids did a great job with that activity; My co-workers were so helpful;* or *My principal really supported me on that issue,* you've planted seeds that produce happier thoughts and feelings in the future.

When you walk into school the following day, your mind will recall what you chose to think in the days prior. Those positive, affirming thoughts will deepen their roots in your mind and become a part of your beliefs and thought system, especially when you share them with others in conversation.

These healthier thoughts will affect the way you view problems all throughout the day. When a student is off-task, your mind will be full of positive recollections and you will be less likely to get discouraged than if you'd been mentally replaying negative thoughts about that student.

Replacing negative thoughts doesn't have to mean being unrealistic and repeating mindless platitudes to yourself. You don't have to grin and repeat, "I love this job more and more every day!" when you feel the opposite (although there is solid research that shows these affirmations can help you internalize a positive perspective, even when you don't yet buy into it.)

Many times, replacing thoughts means simply noticing the good things as they happen. It means paying attention to the small wins, and focusing your mind on them. Even when a lot of stuff is going wrong, you can train your mind to pay more attention to what's going right:

There were a lot of challenges today, but rather than re-hash them, I'm going to choose to remember how I finally got that stack of graded papers entered into the computer. I got to see one of my favorite former students in the hall and give her a hug. And Ms. Samuel and I had a good laugh during our co-planning. There were definitely some great moments today.

Replacing negative thoughts with positive ones can also involve examining the evidence: Is the negative thought really true?

Choosing a positive outlook is far from being mindlessly cheerful despite all evidence to the contrary: usually the facts of reality do not support our negative thoughts. Much of our pessimistic thinking is based on assuming the worst, and predicting that whatever bad thing that's happening will impact us on a much larger scale and for a longer period of time than it actually will.

You can replace these thoughts with positive thinking that is actually far more realistic:

I feel like this new teacher's guide is impossible for me to ever figure out and is going to make it so much harder for me to teach this subject from now on. But the truth is that I will figure it out eventually—I've always been able to manage new teaching manuals—and I'm sure I'll find a work-around that makes this feasible. It won't be this hard forever. Soon, I'll fit the new outlines into my teaching style.

You might choose the "replace" strategy for thoughts that can't easily be dismissed:

I feel like I'm being so lazy all the time. But, I know the truth is that I'm not lazy. I get a lot of things done and I'm an accomplished person. It doesn't seem like I got much done today, but I did do x, y, and z, and I'm choosing to focus on that. Also, my worth isn't determined by my productivity. I don't have to work to the point of exhaustion to feel satisfied with what I've accomplished.

Replacing negative thoughts with more accurate and positive sentiments is the most powerful way to prevent unwanted thoughts from returning. It's also one of the most important strategies you have for managing your mindset—so important that I've devoted the entire third section of the book to it.

For now, though, try experimenting with these 4 strategies for dealing with unwanted thoughts (dismiss, distract, reject, replace). Notice when each one is helpful, and when each just isn't effective for you.

You might find that one strategy works well for awhile, and then stops working, and so you lean on another. This is very normal, and demonstrates the importance of having a wide range of options for yourself so can choose whatever feels most helpful in each scenario.

As you practice these strategies, they'll become like second nature, and you'll know which tool in your thought-work toolbox to reach for in various challenging situations.

4

Choosing a response to
your emotions

Our minds attach feelings to each event in our lives, and this attachment is very powerful. When you look back on your past, you'll notice that you can recreate feelings by thinking about bygone events: warm, happy feelings of satisfaction from a time when a student thanked you, or feelings of annoyance when a student disrupted a lesson.

For the most part (with traumatic experiences as a notable exception), the emotions we feel when recalling memories are a result of our thoughts about those memories. When an event occurs, our beliefs and thought system determine our reaction to it. The way we *think* about it then becomes the way we *feel* about it.

How thoughts lead to feelings

Let's say you're in the middle of teaching your class and there's a knock on your door. With no warning, you've gotten a brand new student. He has a grouchy look on his face and refuses to greet you or even make eye contact when you introduce yourself.

Your belief system and automatic thoughts may include ideas like these:

I should not be interrupted during lessons. I can't possibly take any more students because this class is already overcrowded and too hard to handle. This student is clearly uncooperative and a troublemaker. He's going to make my job harder. I can't believe this is happening. This year just keeps getting worse and worse.

When you think those thoughts—even if you're not aware they're running through your head—you give rise to various emotions like irritation, anxiety, mild panic, exhaustion, and anger. The process of emotion following thought can happen in the blink of an eye, so quickly and automatically that you may not even be aware that your thoughts were the catalysts for your feelings. And yet, your negative emotions arise largely out of negative thoughts.

If your thoughts about the student are different, your emotions will also be different. Your automatic thoughts might play out this way:

Wow, that was a surprise. Although I'm not prepared for another new student, I can see this kid is very apprehensive and insecure about being here. I want to welcome him as warmly as possible to let him know he's safe in our room. Though I'm not thrilled about having another student in this class of 32, I know he has something special to contribute, and he can accomplish great things with us here. Rather than dwell on this new challenge and make myself feel overwhelmed, I'm just going to get the student settled and get right back to teaching my lesson.

Thoughts like this will probably result in feelings of mild annoyance (but not rage) and after a few moments, it's pretty easy to downregulate your nervous system back to a neutral or more relaxed state.

Remember, an external event cannot create feelings of indignation, frustration, or rage. *Your thoughts and beliefs about the situation create those feelings.*

That's why getting a new student might barely break your stride one day, but on a different day, it throws you off completely off-kilter. When you're in a healthier place mentally, a setback doesn't generate those extreme thoughts and correspondingly extreme emotions.

> **This is a very important and empowering concept, because it means you have some control over how you feel. No person or situation can *make* you feel upset. The stress reaction that you experience can be increased or decreased based on the thoughts and feelings you generate.**

You can test this idea out the next time you start to notice a bad mood setting in. See if you can make the connection between your thoughts and feelings. For example:

I feel so irritable right now—everything is getting on my nerves. Why might that be—what thoughts have I been thinking? Well, I was just making a mental list of everything I did for that student's family and replaying how all they did was ask for more favors. No wonder I don't feel like being around people right now, when I was so focused on the thought that everyone just takes, takes, takes from me all the time!

Can you see how this is different than concluding that your irritability is due to a parent who keeps making demands? A student's parent asking you to do something can't create a bad mood in you. Dwelling for a long period of time on how unreasonable the parent is, how parents want too much these days, how you're constantly being asked to do more than you possibly can, and making a mental list of all the other requests you've heard lately? *That* can put you in a bad mood for sure!

Here's another example of how to make the connection between your feelings and the thoughts that preempted them:

I don't feel like doing ANYTHING right now. What could have caused that? Let's see what I've been thinking about today... Well, I've spent a lot of time this morning worrying about how little sleep I've gotten the last few nights and how much I have to do. Instead of just lying in bed relaxing when I woke up in the middle of the night, I counted how few hours of sleep I've been getting lately, and started feeling agitated, so it became impossible to go back to sleep. I also complained to a couple different people this morning about how much I need sleep, and was doing mental calculations about how much I'd need to sleep this weekend to make up for it. I think between the actual lack of sleep and worrying about the lack of sleep, my body's worn out, and that's why I have no energy. The thoughts I have about losing sleep are definitely not re-energizing!

This kind of self-examination can give you power over unwanted feelings. Your moods may feel less mysterious and easier to understand, which means you can be more gentle and compassionate in your self-talk. A bad mood or low energy doesn't mean something is wrong with you: it's possible that you've been mentally processing too many de-energizing thoughts.

Using negative thoughts as clues to what we need

As soon as you notice feelings of unhappiness, dread, anxiety, or other unwanted emotions creeping in, start thinking about what you've been thinking about.

In this way, your feelings can be a very beneficial tool, providing insight into your unconscious beliefs and automatic thought system that you might otherwise fail to notice.

Negative or stressed out feelings can also provide a clue that your mind is not focused on the present. If you're feeling anxious or worried, it may be that your thoughts are centered on what might happen in the future; if you're feeling frustrated or sad, you might be rehashing something from the past that can't be changed.

When you experience an unwanted emotion, ask yourself: *What have I been thinking about? Something that already happened and I am powerless to do anything about? Something that has not yet happened and cannot be controlled by me in this moment?*

If either one is the case, return your mind to the present moment using the *dismiss, distract, reject,* or *replace* strategies explained previously. Clear your head of those thoughts, and your positive emotional state will eventually return.

Make no mistake: I'm not suggesting that everyone should be happy and unstressed at all times. Feelings such as melancholy and despondence are normal. We don't need to interpret sadness or anger as inherently bad feelings.

And, we'll all experience situations that are deeply upsetting. It's not realistic to expect yourself to feel carefree in those moments, and you may want to aim for a more neutral experience rather than a positive mood during those times.

On a scale of 1 to 10 (with depression at a one and ecstatic joy at a 10), you may find it helpful to aim for a 4, 5 or 6 each day. This is particularly true when you have a stressful job or home life, or are experiencing ongoing trauma. Expecting yourself to have the energy and mood of a 9 or 10 on a daily basis may just make you feel like there's something wrong with you and you "should" be happy.

Even though someone else always has it worse, *your pain and suffering is valid.* You are allowed to be sad, discontented, and angry. You do not have to "suck it up" or "just deal with it because that's how life is."

That's just shutting off our emotions and denying how we feel. Telling ourselves that everything is fine when it's clearly *not* fine can disconnect us from our intuition and inner knowing, so that we're left feeling ungrounded.

Instead, validate your own pain. It feels real to you, and pushing it away can cause you to miss an important signal from your body that things need to change. Sitting with your discomfort feels unpleasant, but it's a healthier coping strategy than gaslighting ourselves into believing we should be unbothered at all times.

As Glennon Doyle says, *all* feelings are for feeling. We are not responsible for pushing away any trace of sadness or anger. Those feelings can be the impetus for us to fight against injustice and advocate for better living and working conditions. Feelings that seem "bad" can motivate us to leave toxic relationships, jobs, and home environments.

Rainbows, lollipops, and unicorns?

So, all of your feelings are valid, in the sense that you have the right to think and feel any way you want. You do not have to change anything unless and until you're ready.

However, not all thoughts and feelings are helpful or useful in your life. When there is too much sadness, anger, or frustration, you may want to change your thoughts to help shift the emotions you're experiencing.

This can be tricky, because our thoughts and feelings seem to be immutable. An extreme thought (*This situation is totally unacceptable!*) will validate the corresponding emotion (*I'm furious—anyone would be upset in this scenario!*) Your thoughts and feelings reinforce one another, making your reaction seem unavoidable. It's a cyclical pattern which can be tough to break.

The key is to notice the unpleasant feeling and identify the thoughts that caused it, then uncover any dysfunctional idea or belief behind it that's exacerbating the situation. With practice, you'll be able to talk yourself through the unwanted feelings and back into a relaxed, neutral emotional state when you're ready.

According to Sonja Lyubomirsky's research, about 10% of our happiness level is determined by circumstances out of our control. Our genetics determines another 50% of our happiness level.

The implication, therefore, is that you have control over 40% of your happiness level, and that's pretty significant. You can pay attention to the relationship between your thoughts and feelings so that you create and hold onto positive feelings more often.

Wanting to feel good and be happy is far from a selfish pursuit. When you're in a higher emotional state, you treat the people around you better and teach more effectively.

Think back to a time in the classroom when you were in a bad mood: How did you speak to your students? What kinds of activities did you facilitate? How much did you accomplish that day?

Compare that to a time in which you had a positive mental affect: you were probably much more patient and understanding with students' shortcomings, willing to engage in more energy-intensive activities and go the extra mile to help students, and were far more productive in your workday.

For this reason, feeling more happiness and positive emotions benefits everyone around you—especially your students, whose daily classroom experience is largely shaped by the moods you exhibit.

Although it's not possible to feel happy, content, and undisturbed during every moment in life, we can choose to generate healthy outcomes from negative emotions. A loss that brings sadness or injustice that brings anger can help us to create positive change in ourselves and the world.

It is possible to grieve without feeling hopeless. You can be frustrated and disappointed without being overwhelmed and paralyzed with anxiety.

By learning to examine your thought system, you can identify which ideas and processes are constructive and which are not, and slowly begin to replace unhealthy mental habits with more effective ones.

If you're feeling guilty or ashamed about your negative emotions (or about the way you express them), you'll find that these feelings lessen considerably when you know that your identity is not in your feelings. You will have the power to observe your emotions and recognize their source in your thoughts, rather than identify with them and use them to define or condemn who you are.

5

Honoring your body, feelings, and moods

A person's mood (current sentiment or disposition) can change frequently from moment to moment. And for many years, I based most of my actions on exactly that—the way I felt in any given moment:

- If I was in the mood to be friendly to my co-workers, I would; if I felt tired and grouchy, I'd keep my head down and duck into my classroom without speaking.

- If I felt patient with the kids, I'd take extra time to help them understand directions and settle into an assignment; if I wasn't in the mood, I'd give directions one time and insist those who weren't listening figure it out on their own.

- If I felt invigorated and accomplished after school, I'd do something productive like clean out a cabinet; if my mood was low-energy and discouraged, I'd sit at my desk and procrastinate on the internet.

My behavior in each of these examples wasn't a conscious choice. Allowing myself time to go on social media or being extra strict about not repeating directions to students would have been fine if I chose those actions intentionally.

But I wasn't doing them because they were the right choice, or even what I sincerely wanted to do. I did them because I was following my moods.

In retrospect, it's easy to see how my moods often stemmed from my thoughts and mental habits.

Negative thoughts about the things coworkers are doing "wrong" will create emotions of resentment, pride, and anger which prevent us from *feeling like* being collaborative and helpful.

Negative thoughts about our most difficult students create exasperation and hopelessness which make us *feel like* giving up on them.

Because so many thoughts cross through our minds during the course of a day, our moods can change from elated to despondent, from disappointed to excited, and from blasé to furious.

Often these changes occur without warning and even without reason. As a result, it can feel like we're stuck on an emotional roller coaster and unable to stop the ride.

3 reasons not to depend on your moods

In carefully observing and monitoring my feelings over time, I've come to understand a few basic characteristics of moods that have made me cautious about giving into them:

1) Moods often lead us to do what's easiest, rather than what's best.

Your conscious mind will tell you the best decision is to get up early, go to the gym before work, and get all your papers graded after school. However, when you wake up, you'll probably be in the mood to sleep in, eat a few doughnuts, and then return to your couch immediately after school to binge watch a TV show.

Your moods are a base instinct. They will often tell you to do whatever feels good in the moment, regardless of the consequences later on.

2) Moods are often illogical.

Have you ever woken up in a bad mood for absolutely no reason at all? When you went to sleep everything was fine, but in the morning…watch out, world!

Maybe you've felt depressed for no reason; your circumstances are the same as the day before, and yet today, everything feels hopeless and impossible. And you've probably noticed that certain things will make you absolutely furious on occasion, whereas at other times they don't bother you at all.

This could be due to hormonal shifts, physical ailments, or any number of factors that have nothing to do with how you *want* to feel.

Moods don't follow logic. One of the most dangerous things you can do is try to reason based on how you feel: *I feel like an idiot, so I must be one. I feel like this task is insurmountable, so it must be too hard. I feel like things are getting worse, so therefore it's true they'll never get better.*

3) Moods are extremely contagious.

The stronger a person's personality and energy, the more likely it is that their mood will rub off on you. Empaths and highly sensitive people in particular need to be mindful not to confuse other people's feelings with their own.

You can start your day in a pretty good mood, but after just a minute or two in the presence of an extremely angry person, your mood might be thrown off-kilter for the rest of the day. Sometimes crossing paths with a rude or inconsiderate driver on the way to work can shift your mood toward the negative.

Similarly, if you live with someone whose moods are often low or shifting unpredictably, that can impact your mood state and cause you to feel and behave in ways that aren't really true to yourself.

Distinguishing between your moods and intuition

Not being able to trust your moods is different from not being able to trust yourself or your intuition.

For me, the difference between a mood and my intuition is that my intuition tells me what's actually best for me and what I really need. It's the wisest part of myself, and manifests as a deep knowing or a still, small voice.

I might *feel like* staying up late and watching just one more episode of my favorite show—that's a passing mood. But my gut instinct, that knowing deep inside, is saying, "Go to bed now; you'll feel so much better in the morning if you do."

> **My intuition is quiet, and I can feel in my body when I'm doing the right thing. I feel lighter, relieved, more energetic. My intuition often tells me to do things I don't *feel like* doing, but that I truly *want* to do.**

For example, I may not have *felt like* taking on more caregiving responsibilities when my grandmother broke her hip, but I *wanted* to do it. My intuition told me: *This is worthwhile. This is the right thing. You will be glad you've done this when you're finished.*

My intuition usually kicks in during big or emotional decisions. If I ignore it, I may feel a lump in my throat or a tightness in my chest. I interpret this as my body's way of telling me, "This isn't the right course of action for you." Or, a lightness might come over me when I decide to go through with something, and my intuition says, "It might feel hard or scary to do this, but deep down, you *do* want to do it, and you'll be relieved you did."

Following your moods isn't always a bad thing

Making smaller daily decisions that are healthy can feel just as challenging as the big stuff. We're not always going to be in the mood to empty that email inbox or finish that load of laundry.

This can lead to an internal battle: *Should I make myself do it, or not?*

I've found that sometimes it's wise to push through those feelings and get started with the task, anyway. I'll often find myself in a state of flow. My mood shifts on its own as I get the satisfaction of completing the task.

But other times, I try to get started and feel every cell of my body resisting. I've learned from experience that it's usually not worth pushing myself to do something when each moment feels like a struggle. I'll usually be able to do the task more quickly and with less effort when I'm in a different mood.

This is particularly true when the task is very demanding either physically, cognitively, or emotionally. If I'm not in the mood to clean out the garage (physically demanding), design a learning unit (cognitively demanding), or have a serious conversation with my partner about a problem in our home (emotionally demanding), I've found it's generally best to wait for a better mood.

The same is true when the folks around you are in a low mood—wait until that's passed to bring up a dicey subject or make a big request, and you'll likely get better results.

Often the difference between "Ugh, I really don't want to" and "Okay, let's get this done" is a good night's sleep and a satisfying meal. Listen to your body when it's calling you to rest or take care of other needs. When you honor the signals your body is communicating, you're more likely to be in a better mood faster, and the task you were dreading today might feel considerably easier tomorrow.

We are humans, not machines. Therefore our moods, energy levels, emotional states, and physical limitations impact our productivity, and it's good to be gentle with ourselves whenever possible.

> **We can't expect ourselves to knock out every item on a to-do list according to how much we believe we *should* be able to get done in a day. Our bodies will feel differently each day, particularly as we age. Our moods and productivity levels will differ each day, and throughout the day. You may notice an impact from the time of the month, season of the year, or from the weather and temperature.**

The more that you pay attention to how these external factors impact your natural moods, the more you can anticipate your high energy and low energy times, and work with your body instead of against it.

The mind-body connection

Richard Carlson, Ph.D., reminds us that feelings vary according to natural mood cycles. It's perfectly normal to have lower moods and higher moods which are closely connected to your physical state. When you're tired, hungry, sick, or in pain, you're more likely to experience a low mood state in which it's much harder to control your feelings and choose your thoughts.

If you're being led by your feelings because you're out of sorts physically, make sure you address those issues as soon as possible, and in the meantime, be aware of how they affect your decision-making. If you've only slept for four hours each of the last few nights, don't make any major decisions, and consider your fatigue when you combat dysfunctional thinking.

Remind yourself: *I'm not feeling my best right now, and I'm more vulnerable to distorted thoughts and irrational feelings. I'm not going to get too invested in what I'm thinking and feeling. I'll take my presumptions and attitudes today with a grain of salt, because they're probably not going to be typical of me.*

Even though the focus of this book is on cognitive habits, the mind-body connection is extremely important and should always be factored in.

Any of type of physical discomfort (most commonly fatigue and hunger) can cause you to become more irritable and irrational. You may feel unable to make decisions, or feel compelled to make them quickly because the problems seem overwhelming and urgent.

Whenever you're at an especially low point in your mood cycle, you can choose to make allowances for yourself and simply wait to decide on a course of action.

However, this has to be a conscious choice, because when you're in a frustrated or angry mood, you often feel the need to fix everything *right now.* This urge is normal but erroneous, because we rarely solve problems effectively when we're experiencing bad moods.

It's wiser to take your mind off whatever's bothering you and let your natural mood state return. Eat something healthy, get some exercise and rest, and take care of yourself.

When you're in a better mood, problems will seem less important and you'll hold them in the proper perspective. New solutions and ideas will come to you because you're thinking clearly and no longer feeling overwhelmed by the magnitude of the issue at hand.

Sometimes you can't avoid making decisions and taking action during low mood periods, but try not to push yourself to do more than is absolutely necessary. Low moods often pass within a matter of hours or even minutes (much faster than what we assume while we're stuck in them.)

Your problems will still be there when you're in a higher mood, only then, you'll be better prepared to handle them.

How to follow wisdom rather than moods

Doing whatever you're in the mood for can lead to procrastination, careless decision-making, unhealthy choices, and other counter-productive behaviors. The opposite of being led by your feelings is being led by wisdom.

Joyce Meyer has said, "Wisdom always chooses to do now what it will be satisfied with later on." When you're tempted to give in to a random mood, stop and think: *What course of action will I be satisfied with later? What's the best choice for me in the long run?*

Living by wisdom is easiest if you put your thoughts in check *before* they develop into feelings. So, let's take a look at how the strategies of dismiss, distract, reject, and replace can all work together to help you choose wise thoughts and overcome your moods.

Let's say you've been pressured into heading up a committee to oversee the school science fair. You've worked around seventy extra hours over the past few months to put together an incredible event, even though your district wouldn't fund it and you had to practically beg your colleagues to help out.

The night of the fair, you miss your own child's soccer game and show up at school to discover that no other faculty members are there to support you. You're left to run the entire evening by yourself...for the twenty families that actually showed up.

Feelings of frustration well up inside and you're nearly shaking with anger. You feel like quitting or transferring to another school where you won't have to do everything yourself and can get some support.

The idea that all your hard work was for nothing keeps floating around in your mind. You complain throughout a late dinner with your partner, and are so wrapped up in your own thoughts that you barely pay attention to your daughter as you put her to bed. When you lie down that night, sleep becomes impossible as you lay there ruminating endlessly on how overworked and under-appreciated you are.

Here's how you can use *dismiss, distract, reject,* and *replace* to help you find thoughts that feel better:

*Tonight was really disappointing. My colleagues and the parents didn't show much support. However, these thoughts are not serving me well. It's not helpful for me to lay in bed all night thinking about how angry I am; I'm punishing only myself and will end up being even more irritable tomorrow because I'm tired. The wise thing to do is **reject** these thoughts that my work was all for nothing.*

*The truth is, the parents who showed up were really appreciative of my efforts, and the smiles on the kids' faces told me they were happy to show off their hard work in science. I'm going to choose to **replace** these negative thoughts with thoughts about how well the science fair actually went with the people who did attend, because I want to be able to sleep tonight. In the morning when I get to school, I can create a plan for preventing this from happening again.*

*But for now, I'm going to make sure my last thought of the night about the science fair is a positive one, and then I'm going to **dismiss** any thoughts on the subject that happen to reoccur. I'm going to read a few pages of this novel to **distract** myself and then get a decent night's rest.*

Chances are good that the problem will seem less pressing and all-consuming in the morning, and you'll be able to handle it with a level head.

Here's another example to consider. Let's say your principal criticized you, and you haven't been able to think about anything else. All afternoon you've been in a bad mood and gave the kids busywork instead of actually teaching because you couldn't concentrate on the project you were supposed to complete with them.

You tried to take your mind off it at lunch and ended up crying in the bathroom. You tried venting to three coworkers and all that did was make you angrier. At this point, your head hurts and you feel sick just thinking about it.

Can you identify the process in this hypothetical situation where you lost control?

First, you allowed negative thoughts to continue unchecked in your mind. These thoughts created overwhelming feelings and emotions which made it even harder to stop your unwanted thoughts.

This continued, and a physical reaction to stress was created in your body, firmly entrenching you in the low mood that had been building all day.

But as soon as you recognize what's happening, you can choose different thoughts that will create better feelings:

It's unhealthy for me to focus on how angry I felt when my principal offhandedly made that remark. This isn't as important as it feels: my sense of worth doesn't come from what my principal thinks. I KNOW I'm making a difference with my kids.

The wise thing to do is not let my feelings get me discouraged, and decide to change my thinking so that I feel better. I'm going to go for a run and get some fresh air to clear my mind.

While I'm outside, I'm going to choose to think about that moment today when James finally understood how to multiply fractions, and how excited he was. What can I do tomorrow to support him in that?

I want to think about a really engaging math activity I can use, and later, I'll check online for some ideas to get myself looking forward to tomorrow's lesson. If the thought about my principal returns, I'm going to totally ignore it and refocus on my hunt for some cool math ideas.

Here's what the mind is doing in that example:

- Recognize the thought as harmful
- Notice any untruths or exaggerations in the thought
- Consciously reject it
- Speak truth that opposes the harmful thought
- Choose a replacement thought
- Engage in a positive, distracting activity
- Dismiss any further unwanted thoughts

The strategies of *dismiss, distract, reject,* and *replace* can be applied in lots of different ways. You'll notice the first restructuring example I gave here about the science fair is more formulaic; the second example about the principal takes a more organic approach.

There is no one right way to do this, and you can restructure your thinking using many different techniques. And of course, you can couple your reframing with taking action, and directly address problems with the people involved. Acceptance and change can go hand in hand!

As you experiment with different approaches, you'll find a number of them that work best for your personality.

Practicing self-compassion when you slip up

While our moods can be a major influence on our lives, I hope you can see now that they're far less important than we often make them out to be.

> **Moods are not necessarily reliable, logical, or based on what's good for you in the long run; they stem mostly from your thoughts. If you've been thinking distorted thoughts, your feelings are probably going to be distorted, too. If you don't like your mood, examine the thoughts that may have helped create it.**

This is a lifelong practice. There will be many times when you don't *feel like* being positive and responsible. Choosing to trust your intuition and live by wisdom rather than your mood is not a final decision you can make once and for all; it's a daily, moment-by-moment choice.

I used to get frustrated with myself: *I just decided yesterday that I wasn't going to do this anymore, and now here I go again!* With time I came to understand that it's not possible to achieve mastery in this area and always make wise, intuitive decisions.

We can only take each choice as it comes and do our best to respond wisely. When we follow our moods, berating ourselves afterward just compounds the dysfunctional thoughts and low mood state. Instead, we can acknowledge what happened and choose to move forward, being compassionate and forgiving of ourselves.

You don't need a new day, week, month, or school year to have a "fresh start." Your choices about what to think and how to behave are happening every moment you're awake. If you don't like a choice you made five minutes ago, you can make a different choice now in this moment, and resume your forward progression.

PART TWO:

CREATING NEW MENTAL PATTERNS

6

Replace self-criticism with self-acceptance

Most people have an ongoing internal monologue or conversation playing in their minds. In movies and television, this is sometimes depicted by having the main character do a voiceover narration that tells the audience what they're thinking and feeling.

I recently found out that a small percentage of the population doesn't think in words and full sentences, but rather in images. I have a friend like this, who thinks in images and does not have an inner dialogue or monologue. She told me when she watched a show in which the audience was privy to the character's internal narration, she thought that was something completely made up for television!

Regardless, this sort of running commentary on what's happening around us is quite common, and is known as "self-talk". If you're a person who thinks in images rather than words, your self-talk may work differently than what I describe in this chapter, but the underlying principles are the same.

Most of us identify with the thoughts that appear in our minds, whether they're words or pictures, and we assume that our thoughts are true and accurate. However, self-talk is colored by our mindset.

How self-talk affects your perception

Self-talk includes lots of automatic thoughts that we've reinforced over the years by paying attention to them and attaching importance. The automatic thoughts pop up without us consciously thinking or even noticing them.

When faced with a challenge, your automatic self-talk might be, *This is too hard. I shouldn't have to do this. There's no way I'll be able to get this done.*

When someone provides constructive feedback, your self-talk might include the thoughts, *They don't like me. They think I did a horrible job. I'm so bad at this!*

Thoughts like these might enter your mind on such a regular basis that you have no idea they're occurring.

Your automatic self-talk is a fundamental part of how you think and feel. In part, that's because we grant more credence to our own thoughts than to those of others. We've trained ourselves to think critically about other people's ideas when they contradict what we know to be true. But if that outlandish opinion comes from our own automatic thoughts, most of us tend not to question it.

It's difficult to critique and analyze our own thoughts because our reality is shaped by the way we think. So instead of being objective, we simply accept whatever we think as truth.

It's not hard to imagine what would happen to your self-esteem if someone was following you around 24 hours a day, pointing out everything you've done wrong and why your life is never going to get any better. Yet that's exactly what happens to some of us—we become our own worst critics, proclaiming a never-ending, scathingly bad review of life that becomes a self-fulfilling prophecy.

Most of the feedback we hear about our performance on any given day comes from our own thoughts. We tell ourselves, *That was dumb. Why'd you do it that way? You should do it differently.*

Many of us say things to ourselves that we would NEVER say to another person: *I'm such an idiot. I have no self-control. I'm a bad teacher.*

If you repeat that type of self-talk, it quickly becomes ingrained in your thinking patterns. Negative thoughts become a part of you, and you internalize the idea that you are, in fact, a loser who sucks at life. You believe your own hype and become convinced that the products of your distorted thinking are true and accurate. Self-doubting thoughts become a part of your belief system.

Therefore, as you learn to address negative thought patterns, the best place to start is with the way you think about yourself.

Watch your language

You can use cognitive restructuring strategies (such as *dismiss, distract, reject,* and *replace*) to change your thinking patterns. A supplementary technique is to replace extreme language with more accurate terms.

Words like *never, always, horrible, awful, worst, impossible, hate, unbearable,* and *unbelievable* are usually exaggerations that cause you to view a situation and yourself in a worse light than necessary.

Instead, try choosing words that aren't so dramatic and final, such as *rarely, usually, challenging, difficult, tough, dislike,* and *surprising.*

An internal monologue that says, *"I hate dismissal duty—I can't believe I'm being forced into a complete waste of time! I can't stand it out here for another second!"* is more likely to create feelings of stress than, *"I really dislike dismissal duty. It's hard for me to stand out here sometimes when I have so many other things to do."*

This seems like a small change, but replacing extreme terms is a really important strategy if you're prone to panic or anxiety attacks, or even just assuming the worst case scenario.

If you pay close attention to your word choice, you'll notice how influential it is on how you feel and what you think later on. Rephrasing your thoughts in a way that's more rational will keep you from getting so worked up, and prevent your thoughts and emotions from spiraling out of control.

Another reason why using less extreme language is important is because it gives you a sense of control and empowers you to change the situation.

If you think something is really awful, you'll probably waste a lot of time thinking about how awful it is rather than expending your energy on problem solving.

Repeatedly thinking about how bad things are can cause you to become convinced that you can't stand the situation and it will never improve. Feeling that you have no control or hope for improvement leads to depression and other severe, desperate emotions.

Choosing less extreme language gives you control: it reminds you that the situation is not unbearable and it won't last forever.

Another technique is to turn negative statements into a question and call to action. Instead of stating dysfunctional thoughts as facts (*I'm never good enough at this*), try asking yourself questions that lead to improvement (*What can I do to help myself improve in this area? Is there another approach I can try?*)

Use pervasive negative thoughts as inspiration for change:

Wow, I just keep thinking about how hard it is for me to get the kids to pay attention during instruction. Instead of telling myself how bad I am at classroom management, what can I do to be more effective? Is there something

I can read or someone I can talk with to learn new strategies? What changes can I experiment with to help me learn and grow in this area?

Building awareness: pay attention to your feelings and conversations

It can be difficult to counter negative self-talk when you don't even realize it's happening. As you're building awareness of your internal monologue and self-destructive thought patterns, pay attention to two factors: how you feel and what you say aloud.

You'll recall from the last chapter that your feelings give you clues to what you've been thinking about: if you feel bad, you've probably had some negative thoughts.

The things you say to other people are also windows into your thinking. Sometimes it's easier to notice the self-deprecating comments that are shared out loud than the automatic self-talk that runs endlessly in your mind.

Practice not undermining yourself in front of others. This is especially important in a professional setting because broadcasting your flaws can damage credibility.

Most of your colleagues have never actually gone into your classroom and seen you teach; the main way they determine whether you're effective or not is based on appearances—your class' behavior in the hallway, the bulletin boards outside your door, and the way you present yourself.

There's no reason to announce loudly at a staff meeting, "I can't control these kids; they just don't listen to me," or "I'm so disorganized—I can't find the paperwork I was supposed to turn in." Speaking negatively about your faults causes others to see those flaws more clearly and predisposes people to view you in a negative light.

More importantly, you should avoid talking badly about yourself because it poisons your own mind with negativity. Anytime you hear criticism—from others or from yourself—it has the potential to be extremely disheartening and lead to more negative thoughts and feelings.

You can't control whether someone else talks badly about you, but you can certainly avoid speaking disapprovingly about yourself. Don't validate your self-deprecation by speaking those thoughts out loud or even by allowing them to stay in your mind: dismiss, distract, reject, replace.

Developing true self-acceptance

Ultimately, the goal is to accept yourself without stipulation, simply because you're *you* and you have to live with yourself. Don't make yourself earn self-acceptance. Don't base your opinion of yourself on how you act or what you accomplish.

You're stuck in your own mind and body as long as you're alive, and if you want that to be an enjoyable experience, come to terms with who you are. You have just as much value as every other human being, simply because you exist!

Your confidence can't be derived from your character or what you've *done*—that's a recipe for frustration, because you won't always behave and achieve the way you want. You cannot be the person (or teacher) you'd like to be 100% of the time, and if your self-image is based on your actions, those times when you fall short will cause you to feel badly about who you are.

Instead, you can re-train your mind to love and accept yourself unconditionally, no matter how you act. Psychologists refer to this as having an "unconditional positive self-regard." You can also think of it as, "learning to separate your WHO from your DO."

The bottom line is that you don't have to earn acceptance or prove your worth to anyone, even yourself. You don't have to accomplish a set amount of tasks in the day to feel like you've been successful. You don't need a completed to-do list to be valuable.

You are here, alive on this planet, and that in itself is enough.

7

Replace pessimism
with examining evidence

Many of our mental and emotional habits were formed as children, even though very few of us were explicitly taught how to respond to stressful situations.

Instead, we watched what our parents, caregivers, and/or other influential adults did, and mimicked their coping strategies. We still utilize many of these strategies today without realizing it (and often without questioning whether our responses are rational and healthy.)

One of the perspectives you acquired as a child is your explanatory style. Anytime you encounter a challenge or setback, your brain--which is wired for making meaning--instinctively creates an explanation for it.

Your explanatory style might be optimistic, pessimistic, or somewhere in between on the spectrum, perhaps near the point your childhood caregivers were at.

Pessimism is the tendency to see, anticipate, or emphasize only bad or undesirable outcomes and conditions. Optimism is the tendency to look on the favorable side and expect the desirable outcome.

Researchers have established through many studies that people with optimistic outlooks tend to be healthier, live longer, have more successful relationships, and experience more enjoyment in life.

Many people who are pessimists will say they're actually realists. Realism is the tendency to view things as they really are. But as we go through each of these pessimistic habits, I hope you'll see that much of the time when we think we are being realistic, we are actually operating from a very distinct cognitive bias. Reality is usually less extreme than the way a pessimist or so-called realist perceives it.

Let's examine some pessimistic thought patterns that contribute to having a demoralized outlook and stress reaction. Some of these concepts are based on Dr. Martin Seligman's research of pessimistic explanatory styles, and some are based on the research of Dr. David Burns, who named and categorized 10 cognitive distortions. (Other researchers have identified hundreds more.)

I've chosen 5 cognitive biases to focus on in this chapter, selecting the ones that I think are most pertinent to understanding the pessimistic explanatory style in teaching,

If you can identify and replace these types of thoughts as they arise, you'll be on your way to building a more positive and realistic perspective.

How you gained aspects of a pessimistic explanatory style isn't super important; just bring your awareness to how these habits manifest *now* and challenge them. Notice how each example of accurate thinking examines the evidence for or against the pessimistic explanation, and creates a more accurate response.

#1 Over-generalizing: arriving at a conclusion based on too little evidence

Generalizations are okay; our brains naturally look for patterns in the world around us. But a healthy generalization turns into an unhealthy over-generalization when you assume your thoughts are factual (rather than speculation) and/or you generalize from too few instances.

Here are two examples of over-generalizing and more accurate thinking:

Over-generalizing: The last two kids who transferred into my class mid-year had a lot of behavioral issues. Anytime I get a new student now, I immediately worry because I KNOW they're going to be difficult kids. Only unstable parents would transfer their children halfway through the school year.

Accurate Thinking: During my career, I've had 50 or more kids transfer into my classes mid-year. If I stop to think about it, maybe 10 of those kids were really tough cases. So 4 out of 5 transfer kids—the vast majority—haven't given me major problems. I can't accurately generalize something negative about parents from that, and it's not fair of me to make assumptions.

Over-generalizing: At last week's team meeting, we were told that the state is cutting $20 million from our budget next year. At yesterday's meeting, they told us it would be $30 million. Every time we have a meeting, they cut more funds. There's going to be nothing left by the end of the year!

Accurate Thinking: In fairness, we *were* told that last week's announcement was a preliminary figure and that the board would meet this week. They did, and now they've given us an updated figure. Makes sense! The figure will probably change again after the federal numbers are released next month. I know the projected budget isn't going to literally shrink on a weekly basis from now until June, and framing the situation that way in my mind isn't helpful. I'll wait and see what the final numbers are and where the cuts are made before I choose my response.

#2 Permanence: assuming (without evidence) that setbacks and problems will exist forever

This is a quintessential quality of pessimism that can lead to extreme hopelessness and despair. If you don't believe that a situation will ever change, it becomes very difficult to face it each day. You may start to feel there's no point in trying to make things better or even showing up to work.

So, if there is any possibility that things could get better, no matter how small, it's advantageous to acknowledge that possibility. Two examples:

Permanence Thinking: We'll never be able to use technology effectively in our school district. Things change so fast that we're constantly five years behind. We'll never have enough money to buy what we need and no one ever knows how to use the devices and programs properly anyhow, so it's a waste of money.

Accurate Thinking: Technology is changing so fast that it's impossible to predict how we'll be using it in another few years. Devices are becoming more and more affordable, so it's possible that our situation will improve. Plus, we have a lot of new hires in our district that are innovative and tech-savvy. Just because we don't presently have a lot of technology and aren't utilizing what we have very well, doesn't mean it will always be that way.

Permanence Thinking: This student is so far behind that he's never going to catch up. I can't do anything for an eighth grader who can barely speak or read English! He's going to have to spend every day just sitting in the back of my room using language learning software on the computer.

Accurate Thinking: This student is far behind now, but he could potentially make significant growth this year. Kids who don't speak the language at the beginning of the year are often holding natural conversations with their peers in English by June. It's unlikely that he'll be reading on grade level by then, but he's hardly an impossible case. His English will probably improve incrementally each week that he's in our school. The efforts I make to help him do make a difference.

#3 Catastrophizing: magnifying negative aspects and minimizing positive ones to assume the worst

The root word here is "catastrophe," and this cognitive distortion causes you to view every problem in exactly that light.

Similar tendencies are sometimes known as filtering (as in, filtering out everything good and only focusing on the bad) and maximizing/minimizing (as in, maximizing the negative and minimizing the positive.)

This type of habit causes you to ignore or disregard the evidence that good things are happening, and over-focus on what's wrong.

Catastrophizing: My presentation during the staff meeting was terrible. I messed up on that second slide and it was really embarrassing. I should have rehearsed more. I should have corrected it. All I can think about was that second slide and how dumb I sounded!

Accurate Thinking: The presentation actually went well—I shared the information on every slide (except one) exactly the way I practiced it. Most people didn't even notice my mistake. At least four people gave me compliments afterward. It takes guts to stand up in front of a group of peers and talk, and I'm glad I faced the challenge.

Catastrophizing: This group of kids is driving me crazy. They never listen no matter what I do. I've tried everything and nothing works. They're terrible! I can't wait until this year is over.

Accurate Thinking: Not every minute of every day is awful with these kids. Some days are better than other days. Some things I've tried have been more successful than others. There ARE some moments when I think I'm getting through to them. The vast majority of kids are making progress, even if getting them there is often a frustrating process. Growth *is* happening in lots of ways.

#4 Polarized thinking: perceiving everything as either perfect or a failure, with no in between

Thinking in black-or-white terms—without acknowledging any gray area—is a typical outcome of catastrophizing.

A person who tends toward polarized thinking often has perfectionistic tendencies, and will view situations as either entirely good or entirely bad.

Most educators I've observed with this habit are harder on themselves than anyone else; they can acknowledge partial success of their colleagues, for example, but condemn themselves for not having reached mastery in every area.

Polarized Thinking: Today was a debacle. I had a surprise walk-through observation during a totally chaotic moment. This entire day was lousy and I just want to crawl under the covers until tomorrow.

Accurate Thinking: The walk-through didn't go the way I would have liked, but that was two minutes out of my whole day. They caught me at a bad moment. The kids were actually pretty on-task for most of the morning and even finished those research projects that I'd been anxious to get done for weeks. That was a major accomplishment! One less-than-perfect observation doesn't have to mean the whole day is ruined, and it certainly doesn't mean I'm a failure.

Polarized Thinking: This unit of study is so stupid. There's no reason that kids in this grade level should have to learn about these concepts. The students aren't ready and it's too difficult. The next two weeks are going to be so boring and hard and the kids are just going to fail the test, anyway. I wish we could throw this whole curriculum out and do something else.

Accurate Thinking: I don't think this unit of study is appropriate for our students, but there *are* some good aspects of our curriculum. If I can get through this unit as painlessly as possible (maybe by looking for some cool supplementary materials online?), we can move on to the next unit which the kids and I actually enjoy and understand. These two weeks will be over before we know it.

#5 False helplessness: assuming (without evidence) that you are powerless over a situation

This is a very common mindset among teachers because we are often disempowered by leadership and legislators who hold us accountable for factors beyond our control.

However, if we internalize a sense of false helplessness, we lose faith in our own ability to create change. Watch out for this! The ability to make a difference is a core belief for most teachers, so stripping ourselves of it can be extremely disheartening.

False Helplessness: The district requires me to give these dumb assessments once a week. This takes time away from my teaching, stresses the kids out, and doesn't improve their understanding. I hate not having any control over how I teach and not being able to use my professional judgment.

Accurate Thinking: I'm not allowed to decide whether to give these assessments, but I *am* allowed to decide how to review the answers with students. The questions themselves are pretty well written, so I can try some different ways of using them in my instruction so that they're actually a meaningful tool for review. I want to take advantage of every area in which I do have some control over my teaching. I'm sure I can make *something* good come out of this.

False Helplessness: I'm hopelessly behind on grading. This pile of papers will be impossible to get through. There's no way I can do it AND do everything else that needs to be done. I don't even want to start because hours of grading will barely make a dent.

Accurate Thinking: I don't have to assess every paper in this stack— I'm only required to take two grades per subject each week. So, I won't formally assess most of this work, and I'll grade three sets of assignments every day after school this week until I'm caught up. I can also think about ways to create less written work that needs to be graded. For the most part, I have the power to choose the number and type of assignments given and the way they're assessed. This situation is not totally out of my hands.

The root of burnout

Did you recognize yourself in any of these scenarios? It's likely that each time you've experienced a pessimistic explanatory style, you assumed you were "just being realistic." You had convinced yourself that the way you perceived things was factual!

This is because you hadn't yet paid attention to your biases and cognitive distortions. You hadn't examined the self-talk that colors everything you see.

Challenging your pessimistic thought patterns means letting go of cognitive distortions and choosing to see things as they really are. This is absolutely key to preventing teacher burnout.

I would venture that almost every teacher who quit the field due to stress felt that their efforts to educate children had been rendered ineffective, the situation would never improve, and they were helpless to do anything about it.

Pervasive, permanent, and powerless—these are the hallmarks of a pessimistic explanatory style!

Your school system may be extremely dysfunctional, but your perspective on your role will determine whether you feel courageous and accomplished, or discouraged and defeated.

How do some teachers cheerfully give their all day after day in the most troubled and challenging schools?

They have optimistic explanatory styles. They believe that good things are happening and worth focusing on, that problems will not last forever, and that their own efforts are making a positive difference.

The optimist sees setbacks as situation-specific, temporary, and changeable.

How to counter your pessimistic explanations

When you find yourself tending toward a pessimistic explanatory style, stop and examine more of the evidence. Is the situation really a *total* failure, or is there some good in it? Is it possible that the situation may not be the way you perceive it and there's an alternative explanation?

One question that's been very helpful for me is, "What else might be true?"

For example, it's possible that a student is tardy to class every day because they and their caregivers don't value education and have no respect for me as the teacher. That might be true. But what else might be true?

It might be true that the caregiver works a night shift and has trouble getting the kids ready first thing in the morning.

It might be true that the student is responsible for getting siblings to their schools/classrooms, creating a delay.

It might be true that the family's transportation situation has become unreliable.

Any of these situations might be true, which helps me get curious rather than judgmental about what's going on. Considering other possibilities allows me to enter a conversation with the student and caregiver with a genuine desire to truly understand so that I can help find a solution.

Avoid rushing to judgment if that's going to lead to defeatist, pessimistic, de-energizing thoughts. Admit that you don't know for sure if a situation is permanent or hopeless, and refrain from making a negative guess or prediction. Be sure to weed out any extreme language and replace it with more accurate terms.

If you find that your pessimistic explanation IS completely accurate, ask yourself, *Is it useful or beneficial for me to perceive things this way?*

Let's say both the caregiver and student in this situation really don't value education at all, and assert that it's absolutely fine for them to show up to school whenever it's convenient. When I explain all the learning that the student is missing, they shrug it off.

Is it useful or beneficial for me to keep thinking about how disrespected I feel and how off-base the family is? Do those thoughts and judgments empower me to show up each day and do the best possible job for kids?

Just because something is true doesn't mean I have to continue to dwell on it. And, just because it's true doesn't mean it's healthy for me to keep thinking about it.

As another example, imagine a student in your class has a 42% average and the grading period ends on Friday. It could be accurate to think, *Marie is going to fail the class and there's nothing I can do about it.*

But does that thought help you teach your classes with enthusiasm and energy? Does it stir up feelings of compassion toward Marie so you're motivated to help her do better next quarter? Does it make you feel good about yourself and your work as a teacher?

If it doesn't, you can choose not to dwell it. Let the thought enter your mind and pass right back out without attaching any importance or giving it any further thought. Dismiss it, distract yourself, and replace your thoughts with things that are beneficial.

If the subject recurs in your mind, choose to reject it by telling yourself, *That's not helpful and there's no good that can come from me ruminating on that idea. I choose not to think thoughts that aren't contributing to my mental well-being. Moving on.*

You can choose between thoughts that feel good, and thoughts that feel bad. Weigh the different perspectives in your mind ("What else might be true?") and choose a thought that feels better.

8

Replace mental loops with healthy reframing

I had about six weeks of teaching experience under my belt on the day a parent stormed into my Pre-K classroom. I was in the middle of a whole group lesson when I heard the classroom door fly open and a woman yell, "My daughter told me you wouldn't help her open her milk at lunch yesterday. You told her to ask somebody else."

Startled by her loud, accusatory tone but wanting to de-escalate things quickly, I excused myself from the students and stepped to the side to try to have a quiet conversation with this woman I had only met once.

"Yes, I probably did do that," I told her. "We have something called the Three Before Me rule in the classroom. If a child needs help with something that another child can do, then the child should ask three other kids before asking a teacher. Since there are eighteen preschoolers who need their milk opened at the exact same time and only two adults, I've taught the kids how to help one another."

She got about three inches from my face. "*You* are the teacher, *you* are supposed to do things for her and not be lazy! If you don't want to do your job, we should get another teacher in here."

Since then, I've replayed that conversation over and over in my mind so many times, thinking of a million different ways I could have responded, and now all the memories have run together in my mind. I can't recall what I actually said, but I do remember repeating the incident to half a dozen people in an attempt to establish that she was a raving lunatic and I was a competent, caring teacher.

No matter how many people commiserated with me, I didn't feel better about it. That conversation haunted me for a long time and my heart skipped a beat every time someone opened the classroom door for the rest of the year.

Why did that one particular memory stay with me? Maybe because it was so traumatic—that was the only time I ever had a parent embarrass me in front of the class, and it happened when I was an insecure first year teacher.

But mostly, I think I retained that memory because I attached importance; it became a part of who I was. I identified with it.

Rather than seeing her criticism as a misunderstanding, over-reaction, or projection of other experiences onto me, I gave her words credence. I questioned my entire competence as a teacher: *Was the Three Before Me rule the right thing to do? Did I neglect the kids? Was I really lazy?*

This went beyond just examining my teaching philosophy, which is a good practice, particularly when someone brings a problem to your attention. I went further than self-examination, though, and accepted her opinion of me as correct. When I felt tired or took a shortcut in my work, I would hear her voice playing in my head and think: *She's right, I am lazy.*

Each time this happened, the root of shame grew deeper. Repeatedly replaying critical thoughts in my mind and rehearsing what I could have done differently weakened me mentally and even physically at times. The confrontation was over, and I didn't have any further problems with that parent (my aide had been able to explain our philosophy well and appeased her.) But I was still recreating that past stress through my thinking.

Constructive reframing

What I eventually learned to do was reframe negative experiences and problems. Then anytime they popped into my head, I'd have a constructive framework through which to view them.

Here's an example of a constructive reframing for the situation I just described:

Regardless of her approach and the other factors at play here, I know this parent wants the best possible learning environment for her daughter, and that's my goal, too. We're on the same side, and though I'm going to try to help HER see that, the important thing is that I see us that way, and not as enemies.

She is not the judge of whether I run my classroom effectively and I don't have to feel badly about myself because we didn't see eye-to-eye on a simple classroom procedure. It's a disagreement over the Three Before Me rule, not some life-altering decision that's worth a ton of mental energy.

Her daughter is learning a lot and will make more progress as the year goes on, and that's going to be my focus. This way, all three of us will be happy. I refuse to replay this incident in my mind any longer. I'm choosing to feel good about the way I run my classroom and the way my students are becoming independent learners. We're on a great path.

After you reframe a troubling incident, you become free to simply dismiss it anytime it reoccurs. You empower yourself to say, *Just because a thought comes into my head doesn't mean I have an obligation to think it. I'm not going there. Everything is fine in this moment and there's nothing to stress about.*

This same reframing strategy works with current unresolved problems if you have the tendency to replay and rehearse those, too.

The first thing my mind used to do upon waking was run down a list of every present conflict and problem I had to solve. If there was any tension between me and another person, I'd replay what was already said (and even more pointlessly, envision how things might have gone differently.) I'd start rehearsing in my mind what I'd say when I saw the person next and play out various directions the conversation might take. I'd try to anticipate every possible response or problem that could arise.

This habit went beyond interpersonal issues. If there were any decisions I needed to make (even long-term plans that couldn't be determined yet), I'd hone in on them immediately, mentally rehearsing what I would say and do.

It's important to learn from the past and think about how to respond wisely in the future. But constantly replaying and rehearsing problems is destructive. It can keep you from fully experiencing the present, and make you feel angry, frustrated, and anxious.

When you're feeling any of those emotions, it's your body's signal that your thoughts are no longer healthy and balanced, and it's time to reframe your thoughts:

I don't have to rehearse for the tenth time what I want to say in the meeting today when we discuss whether teachers should take on an extra lunch duty each week. My energy is better spent preparing for today's lessons. I refuse to waste time mentally listing all the reasons why an extra lunch duty would be untenable, and I'm not going to replay the problem in my mind.

I wrote down my important points so I won't forget when it's time for the meeting, and I'll be fully focused on the issue then. Right now, my priority is getting ready for my students.

If you struggle with the mental habits of replaying and rehearsing, practice this process of reframing instead.

Start with the one incident that plagues you the most: the work-related argument or conflict that is most troubling, or that resurfaces in your mind more than any other.

Maybe there's an incident that you constantly upset yourself about, and need to reframe so you can have some peace:

I can't believe I asked my co-worker that insensitive question about when she was planning to become pregnant. I overstepped a boundary and really embarrassed myself...and her!

How can I reframe the incident in my mind so I can stop replaying it?

Well... I did go back to her afterward and apologized. I told her that I would not ask presumptuous personal questions of her again and took ownership of my behavior. I hope that she'll be willing to see that I'm trying now to act from a place of integrity, and over time, I can rebuild her trust and friendship.

I've done everything I can to make things right, and making myself feel bad about it now doesn't change anything. It's time to distract myself and think about something else.

You can also write down your reframing if you want. This can help you remember it and serves as a great reference tool later on. Here's an example:

I'm writing down my new perspective on the way I handled that confrontation with a student so that I can have a better relationship with them. I'll read it to myself before class if I need a pep talk:

I accept that I made the best choice I could under pressure. I also know that I made all conceivable amends afterward. I'm choosing to leave what happened in the past. I will not punish myself by continually revisiting it and imagining how I could have responded better.

I do not expect myself to respond perfectly in every situation. I forgive myself.

Moving forward, I am practicing being slow to anger. I care about this student and am going to think positive thoughts about them so I don't get fed up and overreact again.

I trust that our relationship will grow stronger slowly over time, and I'm willing to do my part to facilitate that. I'm choosing to act from a place of kindness and compassion toward myself and toward my student.

As you train your mind not to dwell on negative thoughts, you'll find that the tendency to replay and rehearse is considerably lessened.

After all, if you don't think condemning, anxiety-producing, destructive thoughts to begin with, there won't be any to replay in your mind later on.

9

Replace old stories
with resilient new ones

Dwelling on the past colors the way we perceive things in the present. It can cause "transference effects," in which you transfer feelings about people from your past to people in your present.

If you hold a grudge against a former student who was disrespectful, you might find yourself being overly harsh with their sibling when they enroll in your class.

If you never forgave a supervisor for patronizing you at a meeting, you might be predisposed to believe that the next person who takes that position will be insensitive, too, and find that you're suspicious of all administrators.

Our inability to process the event, forgive the person or people at fault (including ourselves), and then reframe things in a constructive way can distort the way we view our current challenges.

Your perceptions are repeated in your mind through your automatic thoughts, creating an imprint in your neural circuitry and establishing your emotional habits.

In other words, your perception of the past becomes a part of who you are and creates unwanted thoughts and emotions during present-day situations.

When we can't process an event in a healthy way and move on, we often deal with it by thinking about it even more (trying to work through the offense logically) and talking about it with other people (in the form of gossiping and complaining.) Unfortunately, this can lead us to never letting things go, and holding onto a permanent grudge.

Digging in the bottomless pit

What should you do about really deep-seated issues? What happens if you know your bad mental habits stem from things that happened a long time ago?

You may have encountered experts in mental health who offer step-by-step instructions to help you work through bad memories. Many proponents of psychoanalysis would advise you to investigate what's making you bitter and uncover the problem's source, especially when unwanted thoughts are deeply rooted in incidents that are decades old.

This strategy has been only marginally effective for me; I found that when I first began doing it, I became more self-involved and depressed. I was in counseling throughout my teens and early twenties, and spoke with various psychiatrists, psychologists, and counselors about incidents in my past and how they were affecting my current reality.

Very little of that time resulted in breakthroughs. I spent way too much time thinking about *my* problems, *my* past, and everything bad that had happened to *me*.

All that analysis inadvertently made me feel even more dysfunctional. In spending so much time dwelling on the pain from my past, I attached more power and importance to those thoughts and feelings.

My pain became a part of my identity, and it grew even harder to move beyond it. On some level, I felt like, *This is who I am. It's how I've always been, and how I'll always be. If I let go of "my" past, what will be left of me? If I no longer identify with these patterns, how will I know what to do? Who am I, if I let these behaviors and coping mechanisms go?*

In recent years—now that I'm at a healthier place mentally--I've found that making connections between my current reality and the past has felt more helpful.

For example, I often notice how I am repeating unhealthy patterns I learned from family members, and how sometimes things upset me in my marriage because they trigger a trauma response from early dating experiences when I didn't know how to identify or communicate my own needs.

Making those connections between my present-day reactions and incidents from the past is probably more useful to me now because I've already done so much cognitive-behavioral training and reframing of my thoughts. Now that I'm older, I understand myself better, I like myself more, and I'm more at peace with my own strengths and weaknesses.

Additionally, the personal development work I've done over the years has helped me distance myself from my feelings a bit. I see myself as the watcher of my thoughts, and therefore my reaction to recalling the past is not as emotional or stressful.

There are a tremendous number of experts who agree there is no need to investigate the past for the sake of working through subconscious issues. The concept is virtually unheard of in traditional eastern thought, and didn't become a norm in western culture until about 150 years ago with the research of Sigmund Freud.

Throughout history, most people believed that if you couldn't fully remember something that would be harmful or painful to recall, you should be grateful!

For me, part of the cognitive-behavioral psychology movement's appeal is that individuals are capable of restructuring their own thoughts. Therefore, we're not dependent on someone else to figure out where the thoughts are coming from and why.

This perspective is echoed almost universally by spiritual and religious traditions, which typically recommend that people struggling with unwanted thoughts stay fully present in the moment and/or place their focus on a higher being and purpose rather than constantly introspecting.

In his book *The Power of Now,* Eckhart Tolle explains that the present will bring out whatever we need to know about our past. Therefore, there is "no need to dig into a pit that can never be fully explored."

Additionally, trauma-informed practices teach us to focus on the effects of the trauma rather than the causes of it. Two people can experience the same problem, and one might feel fine while the other is deeply impacted. If we're examining the cause, we might assume this means that both people should have the same reaction, and if one person's okay, there must be something "wrong" with the other.

Being responsive to your own trauma can look like shifting away from *What's wrong with me?* to *What happened to me?* With this framing, you're no longer focusing on your symptoms but on understanding how adverse experiences shaped your coping mechanisms.

I also like the framing of *What's happening with me?* As in, what are you experiencing now in your mind and body, and what supports do you need in order to cope, heal, and thrive?

This is a very different approach than assuming there is something wrong or disordered with you that needs to be figured out and fixed.

Avoiding helplessness

I hope this doesn't sound like I'm advising you to repress your memories and not deal with hurtful things from your past. Talking with a skilled, licensed therapist about specific issues that you haven't dealt with can be very, very helpful.

But in general, a good goal is to focus most of your energy on the element of time you actually have control over: the present.

The past no longer exists, except in your thoughts. Only your memories keep it "alive" and allow it to have any influence on your life. Though incidents in your past may have been upsetting *then*, you don't have to upset yourself in this moment by thinking about them *now*. Your past cannot create pain in the present—but the way you think about your past can.

Whenever you delve into past offenses and problems—in your own mind, when complaining to friends, or when analyzing with a therapist—be aware that you will be bringing up negative feelings. When you recreate the past by thinking very pointedly about it, your body will recreate the stress response in a surprisingly realistic way.

These tense, unhappy feelings will reinforce your belief that you have a reason to be upset ("See how bothered I get just by thinking about it? It's really a huge problem!") In your mind, this will justify all the distressed thoughts you had about the problem and can make you feel a sense of false helplessness.

A victim mentality is amazingly easy to adapt when you spend time investigating your past. Be alert whenever you find yourself falling into negative thought patterns and getting upset about it, and instead consciously avoid the trap of self-pity and helplessness.

You do yourself a disservice by dwelling on thoughts like, *There I go again, acting like my mom did. This is just the way we handle things in our family. I always get worked up and anxious. It's just what I do.*

Reframing your past in a way that feels healthier

Knowing that you have a diagnosis (such as depression or anxiety) or that a problem stems from childhood can cause you to believe unwanted thoughts cannot be helped and will always be there.

Instead, try noticing any polarized thinking that crops up. Pay attention to when you believe that there's just one version of the truth, or one version of what happened. Ask, "What else might be true here? What's another perspective I might not have considered?"

This line of questioning has helped break me out of a helpless or victimized feeling, and also prevented me from demonizing and dehumanizing people whose choices I don't agree with.

There is always more to the story than I have considered, and more than I can ever know. Being mindful of the fact that I can never fully understand why other people have done the things they've done can make it easier to let go of my need to create a coherent story around what happened. Some incidents in our lives will frankly never make sense, and being open to this truth can release us from trying to figure out the impossible.

Also pay attention to when binary thinking creeps in. This is when you're convinced there is a clear right and wrong in a situation that's actually subjective. ("My parents shouldn't have disciplined me in that way when I was young. My parents should have given me this opportunity and support.")

You can then choose to look for the nuance and paradox. ("They made a lot of mistakes, but they also raised me better than their parents raised them. While I wish they had done things differently in these areas, my parents broke several generational patterns in other areas so that I didn't have to unlearn them.")

"Both/and" can be a soft landing place when you're trying to make sense of situations that are hard to reconcile. "That person hurt me, AND they didn't intend to do so or know it was happening." "Their behavior was incredibly harmful AND there were also causes for their behavior that I can empathize with."

I assure you from experience: you have a tremendous ability to shift your moods simply by changing what you are focusing on.

> **You have the ability to see your past differently, depending on the story you tell yourself about it. You can choose a framing of your past that is more nuanced, self-compassionate, and empathetic toward others.**

You can then take control of what you're thinking in this moment by using the strategies you're learning in this book (such as *dismiss, distract, reject,* and *replace*).

> **Remember, even if you identify the root cause(s) of your problems, you'll still need to create change in how you think, feel, and act in the present. Just because you understand *why* you're the way you are doesn't mean you're yet empowered to *change* unhealthy mental habits.**

At some point, you'll need to examine your current mental habits, identifying cognitive distortions and replacing them with healthier, more flexible thoughts.

If you struggle to enjoy the present moment because your mind is always thinking about the past, your professional life may be the perfect area to start working on. Most of our unresolved work-related issues are less deep-seated and painful than events from our personal lives.

Here are some phrases I've found helpful that you might want to use in your own reframing of troublesome past events, whether they happened this morning or years ago:

- *This incident is over. The other person is probably not thinking about me or what happened, and I'm not going to think about it, either. Why should I be burdened with this issue while they're out enjoying life?*

- *I refuse to create pain for myself in this moment by reliving events from my past. I can choose what I want to think about, and I don't want to think about THAT.*

- *I'm choosing to only ruminate on things I have control over. This situation is in the past. I can't change what I said or did back then. I CAN change how I'm thinking about it now, and shift my focus to something productive.*

- *Whatever already happened is done. I'm okay. My life is moving on and my thoughts will catch up with it.*

- *I am not defined by what happened in my past. I've learned and grown since then. I choose not to let the past interfere with my present, my future, and my destiny. I believe there are wonderful things ahead for me. I trust myself to be able to handle whatever comes my way.*

Focus on your past resilience over your past pain

When you feel like giving up on yourself because the issues seem too big to solve, remember how much you've already overcome.

You've already survived childhood and everything you experienced during it. You survived your teenage years, and every experience you had then. You survived every friendship, partnership, and relationship you've had. You survived the first day of school as a brand new teacher. You survived a pandemic.

And now, you're at this place in your life…maybe not where you wanted or hoped to be, but look at all that you've overcome. Notice every single accomplishment that seems minor to you but is actually something that shaped you into the person you are today. Recognize every hardship that could have ended in a much darker scenario.

You. Are. Still. Here.

Find the peace that comes from knowing how much you have adapted in the past, and how many lessons you've learned about what NOT to do and how NOT to live. Think about all the ways you've diverted from the path of negative influences in your life and chosen better, even when it was hard.

Your past resiliency is proof that you are a survivor, that you can keep pressing forward. You have already adapted to circumstances you never could have imagined for yourself.

Practice radical acceptance: this is the life you've lived. This is the person you are. You've already done amazing things, and grown into an amazing human being.

You are becoming wiser with each passing year. You are unlearning old patterns, growing as a person and an educator.

You've already done so much—you can do THIS, too.

Replace taking things personally with a broader view

I once worked with a very sweet woman who was an excellent teacher but quite insecure.

If I didn't smile one morning when she walked in the classroom, she assumed I was mad at her. If the principal failed to recognize her hard work on a committee, she assumed it was because he thought she'd done a bad job.

Her habit of jumping to conclusions always ended up with the situation being about *her*. Without realizing it, she lived in a constant state of paranoia, worrying that every setback was something she was responsible for.

She took every problem personally, no matter how much everyone reassured her that it wasn't her fault.

Though I really liked this coworker, it was a bit exhausting to be around her, because she required others to do constant damage control and provide reassurance.

It's not about you

All of us personalize things we see as problematic to some degree. I sometimes take it personally when teachers I'm coaching are not as receptive as I'd like.

I remember once I had spent a great deal of time creating resources for a teacher and walked into her classroom to deliver them. I was grinning from ear to ear as I held up the stuff I made.

She was sitting with her laptop and barely looked at me. "Just put it on the table. Thanks."

My feelings were a little hurt. Had I done something to upset her? Did I misunderstand what she wanted me to do? What had I done wrong?

I tried to put the incident out of my mind and reassured myself that I probably hadn't caused the problem, but I felt deflated and a little anxious.

I passed the teacher in the hallway later that day and she stopped me. "Hey, Angela, I'm really sorry about this morning. My mom's in surgery today but I don't have any personal leave left so I couldn't be with her, and I'm so distracted. On top of that, the principal said she wanted report cards done by 10 a.m. today instead of tomorrow, which means I had to work on them during class. The buses were late this morning so kids were trickling in for like an hour and acting crazy. It was a *bad* morning."

She sighed. "But thanks so much for bringing that stuff in, I appreciate it."

Wow. There I was, trying to figure out why she was acting coldly toward *me*, and her mom was in surgery. It wasn't about me at all!

Isn't that usually the case? We have no way of knowing all the personal struggles people are going through. Health issues, family conflicts, marital stress, and financial problems are often unknown to us but shape people's very character sometimes.

The same holds true for our students. Children who are disrespectful, obnoxiously attention-seeking, or totally indifferent are not necessarily acting that way *toward you*.

Though your actions and classroom climate affect student behavior, kids respond from all sorts of unimaginable life situations and mental habits. Most students don't have a grasp on metacognition (the ability to think about their thinking) and may have thought processes that create extreme, unpredictable behaviors. Just like adults, kids' cognitive distortions impact the way they think and act.

Students who appear not to like or respect you may actually *want* to connect, but have such unhealthy mindsets or coping mechanisms that a positive relationship with you feels impossible to them.

Even when that's not the case, how they feel about YOU is undoubtedly just one piece of the puzzle, so don't take their behavior personally!

This issue extends beyond relationships: many of us even personalize school policies.

If teachers are suddenly required to clock in daily or are threatened with docked pay if they leave 15 minutes early, a staff member might start worrying that they've been caught not working the full contracted day: *Uh, oh! Did they create that policy because of something I did?*

If a new weekly quiz is supposed to be administered and the data reported on for the district, a teacher might assume it's a personal attack: *They don't trust me to teach the lessons! They think I'm not doing my job!*

Of course, in both scenarios, it's far more likely that the new policies were made because of the actions of dozens of teachers, and probably not even the ones who were worried about it.

It's even possible that the decisions were made for entirely different purposes, such as fulfilling a new federal mandate or aligning with a neighboring district or state that had such policies.

Since there are so many factors at play here, taking school policy personally is a recipe for frustration. You'll be able to respond to the policy and advocate for yourself much more easily if you choose not to interpret the situation as a personal affront against you specifically.

Repeatedly allowing yourself to turn slights and offenses into personal attacks can cause you to become paranoid, defensive, and bitter.

If someone makes an innocuous comment, you'll find yourself jumping down their throat. Your self-talk starts to include thoughts like, *No one appreciates me, everyone takes advantage of me.*

Resentment builds toward the people around you. It's a sneaky downward spiral that has to be stopped right at the root of the problem.

Recognize that the way people treat you is mostly a reflection of how they feel about themselves and their own lives. Then when a colleague or student treats you poorly, *choose* not to take it personally.

Remember, you won't necessarily *feel like* giving them the benefit of the doubt—you will likely feel hurt or angered. But in choosing to eventually land in a place of compassion and non-judgment, you lessen your own suffering.

4 strategies to stop personalizing problems

Personalization is another one of the cognitive distortions identified by Dr. David Burns. It's simply a skewed way of looking at the world, and like the other distortions, can be altered by restructuring your thoughts. Here are five strategies that can help you not take things so personally:

1) Remind yourself that others are busy and often thoughtless in their hurry.

People are thinking about what they need to get done and not about how their actions affect others. And by "people," I mean all of us.

If you've ever inadvertently cut someone off while driving and only noticed the car after it was visible in your rearview mirror, or pushed ahead of someone in line without even seeing them standing there, then purposefully recall those memories when you feel insulted.

Were YOU trying to make an arrogant statement that your time is more valuable than everyone else's, or were you just wrapped up in your own thoughts and oblivious to the present moment?

Assume the same of others.

2) Gather the evidence to see if you can support your conclusion that there's a real problem AND it's about you.

Ask yourself these questions:

- Is this really an issue, or am I creating or overcomplicating it?
- Is there any proof that this incident was truly about me or something that I did?
- Is it possible that the truth will surface on its own and the situation will resolve itself if I don't react immediately?

3) If there is no evidence that you've done something wrong, assume there is no problem unless someone directly tells you there is one.

Working from the assumption that things are fine places the responsibility on others to communicate their own needs. You do not have to be constantly on edge, watching people's body language and reading into their tone to try to figure out what they *really* feel.

Many people with this tendency have developed it as a coping strategy when living with an emotionally abusive or narcissistic family member/partner. They learn to anticipate things other people might get upset about (like food being served cold, or a messy area left in the home) and feel responsible for preventing any potential outburst.

While being hyper-aware of other people's needs and emotions may have helped you survive a difficult or dangerous situation in the past, be aware of how you may replicate those patterns unnecessarily in other relationships.

You do not have to walk on eggshells around your coworkers, for example, making sure everyone is happy with you at all times. If you've done something they don't like, they need to tell you about it. Until then, it's not your problem.

It can be incredibly freeing to entrust people around you to speak up when they want you to do something or have a request. This is their responsibility. You don't have to anticipate their every need in advance and read between the lines about what they may be implying.

4) Work on your own self-awareness.

99% of the things I'm writing about in this book were completely lost on me during my first year of teaching as a twenty-one-year-old. But as I began building awareness of my own distorted thought patterns, I started to recognize those habits in others, too.

Then when people did things that could potentially hurt me, I'd be able to think, *Oh, this person has a problem with preconceived expectations and presumptuous judgments, just like I do! Her words weren't anything against ME; they're a reflection of her own issues!*

In that moment, I'd understand why the person had said or done something offensive and it wouldn't bother me as much. The stronger I became emotionally, the less other people had the power to hurt me.

As the saying goes, "Hurting people hurt people." We can stop that cycle by approaching the situation with more intentionality.

Tell yourself, *Today I will be aware of other people's struggles and not take their behaviors personally if they act in ways that are potentially offensive. I will actively look for ways to help meet the needs of students, colleagues, and parents so they're in a better place emotionally.*

With practice, you'll find that your default response becomes empathy and a desire to understand. For example, you might think: *Wow, my team leader's tone was very short in that email about not having made our copies for this week. She must be stressed out. What can I do to lessen her load? Maybe I could offer to make the copies next week.*

Or maybe: *This parent wants a list of objectives for the lesson I just taught. Instead of feeling like she is attacking me and questioning the value of the activity, maybe I could offer to show her where my lesson's corresponding state standards are listed online. She needs reassurance that her child is making progress and getting prepared for the next grade. I get that. I'll provide her with as many tools as possible to make her feel good about how much her child is learning. I'm glad she cares enough to ask questions.*

11

Replace blame with an
accurate sense of responsibility

Ah, the blame game. It's always been a defining element of our education system, but the more that test score pressure abounds, the more everyone gets drawn into a brutal cycle of finger pointing.

It typically goes like this: employers and college professors blame high school teachers for not preparing students for "real life." High school teachers blame middle school teachers for sending them students who they claim have no self-discipline and can't read well. Middle school teachers blame elementary teachers for the same thing, and elementary teachers in turn blame parents for sending their kids to school without ever having read them a book or taught them to respect adults.

Educators in general blame the community and students for not pulling their weight, but the public and school district tell teachers it's all THEIR fault.

Oh yeah? teachers counter. *Maybe I could do a better job if you paid me a living wage, gave me the supplies I need, and stopped making me spend every moment testing instead of teaching. It's not MY fault!*

There's another factor to add to this complicated equation: the field of teaching tends to attract altruistic, good-hearted people who hope to make a difference. They're there because they want to help kids. Then they're confronted with a massive amount of limitations on their ability to do so—obstacles they never could have imagined as preservice teachers.

Trying to solve all these problems while simultaneously being blamed for them leads many teachers to arrive at one of two demoralizing conclusions: 1) There are too many problems outside of my control and it's impossible for me to overcome them, or 2) I *have* to overcome them at any cost to myself because I'm personally responsible for students who fail to achieve.

In other words, "It's not MY responsibility" or "It's ALL my responsibility."

These two perspectives seem oppositional. But, they're both dysfunctional perceptions of personal accountability.

For that reason, it's possible (and even common) for teachers to swing back and forth between the two perspectives frequently and struggle to find the middle ground.

In this chapter, we'll explore the unhealthy thoughts that go too far in either direction, and look at ways to stay centered with an appropriately accountable mindset.

"It's not *my* responsibility."

The teacher who blame-shifts rarely takes responsibility for their own actions. They have an excuse for every shortcoming: *I didn't understand the teacher's manual so I skipped that lesson. The principal didn't remind us when the forms were due so I didn't turn them in. My students' parents don't return phone calls so I couldn't schedule any conferences. The kids weren't listening during my lesson so I just gave them busywork. Oh, well. What am I supposed to do? I'm "just" a teacher, right?*

Blame-shifters like to surround themselves with others who are equally disempowered. In a process sometimes referred to by psychologists as *colluding,* they round up a group of people who share their cognitive distortions and reinforce them.

The teacher who's in colluding mode relies on a tight circle of self-pitying and/or blame-shifting colleagues, all of whom repeat their dysfunctional perspectives to each other. Typically, one of their favorite topics of conversation is how students refuse to take responsibility for their actions and have no accountability for their work or behaviors. Since colluders surround themselves with people who think like they do, the irony is lost on them.

Colluders often have a particular scapegoat upon which they repeatedly shift blame: *"Isn't this just another example of how our guidance counselor is completely incompetent? No wonder we didn't meet standards last year with his disorganization! And did anybody notice that he was half an hour late to school again yesterday? He's always late. He was sleeping in while we were working our butts off!"*

Notice the over-generalizing and polarized thinking. If someone with a healthy perspective overhears and says, "Um, really? We didn't meet standards because the guidance counselor is late to school a few times a year?," the colluders will probably determine that the outsider just doesn't "get it" or is trying to suck up to administration.

Most of us do slip into colluding and blame shifting on occasion, so don't feel bad if you recognize yourself in these scenarios!

This all ties back to the issue of believing that stress and unwanted feelings are caused by *external* events, rather than impacted by the way you perceive your circumstances. When you believe that the cause of your problems is entirely outside of yourself, you start to feel helpless and disempowered, and believe that you cannot be happy until your circumstances change. Since you think you can't change things, you put all your energy into telling yourself how awful things are rather than working to improve the situation.

Some people have a blame-shifting mentality across every aspect of their lives. But many teachers start their careers feeling idealistic and eager to take on responsibility, and only later find themselves falling into the blame-shifting trap.

Constantly being held accountable for things you cannot control produces guilt and saps motivation. Many teachers live with these feelings for years until one day they snap and say, *"That's it, this is impossible! I give up! It is what it is, I don't care anymore!"* They become jaded and disillusioned, then emotionally detached as a coping mechanism.

I have observed a number of veteran teachers who sometimes *seem* cruel or uncaring, but in fact, were once greatly invested in their students' education and the community as a whole. Their initial dedication and deep desire to create positive outcomes created burnout over time due to limitations of the system they work within. As a result, they go into survival mode, and simply try to "make it through" to retirement.

To be clear, this is not solely a mindset issue. The demands on teachers are increasing over the years, and many veteran educators see a massive disconnect between the current state of the profession and the job they initially signed up for.

That said, all-or-nothing thinking can be *part of* what causes teachers to swing from taking too much personal responsibility in their idealistic youth to emotionally withdrawing later in their careers.

Teachers in this scenario have arrived at the conclusion that they can only make it as a career educator if they stop being so invested in the work. They go to school each day and do what needs to be done, but have little stake in the outcome. Often these teachers are still quite effective at their job because they're so experienced, but they may be feeling miserable on the inside.

They shift the blame for their unhappiness to outside circumstances, relinquish their own personal responsibility, and avoid taking empowering actions that would help them make the best of a tough situation. They survive, but at what cost?

"It's *all* my responsibility."

Being held highly accountable for student achievement can cause you to rebel against that expectation and shift blame to others, but it can also create a different unhealthy mindset, which is too much personal responsibility.

Many teachers hold conscious or unconscious beliefs like: *I'm a bad teacher if any of my kids fail; My value as an educator is determined by my students' test scores; If I don't conduct elaborate projects like the teacher next door, I'm not good at my job;* and *If my classroom doesn't look perfect and run smoothly all the time, it's because I'm not working hard enough—I have to do more!*

This has been especially true in recent years as educational leaders and the media have bombarded us with talk about merit pay, value-added teacher evaluations, and excessive micromanagement and oversight of classroom practice.

But just because you're constantly hearing messages that you're not doing enough, doesn't mean that's true. The more you accomplish, the more folks in charge will pile on your plate. The bar will be continually raised.

So, challenge their inaccurate beliefs just as you've learned to challenge your own! Don't accept their opinions as truth just because someone with a business degree says their research proves it. Refuse to internalize harmful messages that cause you to believe you are completely at fault because 100% of your students are not working on grade level.

Placing too much responsibility on yourself leads to exhaustion and burnout. Eventually it can lead to martyrdom, which becomes a deeply ingrained pattern of behavior.

Teachers who struggle with the martyr mentality usually don't know how it started or even realize it's happened; they just assume it's an occupational hazard that everyone falls into.

The martyr teacher is one who always works 10+ hour days and then takes home a rolling cart full of papers each night. Martyrs may show up to every one of the students' extra-curricular activities on weekends. They are often one of the most valuable members of the faculty, heading up every committee and never saying no.

The well-intentioned martyr tells themselves that they're doing a good thing for students, but complains about the unsustainable workload and says they feel taken advantage of.

The martyr ruminates on how much they're sacrificing, yet feels compelled to give incessantly until there's nothing left to give. The martyr appears to love their job, but also loves the feeling of being needed, and can easily get trapped in patterns of approval-seeking and people pleasing.

A variation of this is the teacher with a martyr *complex*. This person might work excessive extra hours (telling everyone around them, "I have so much to do, I'm working until dinner every day this week!") or they might scrape by doing the bare minimum ("I can never get ahead, so forget it, I'm coming in late and leaving early from now on.")

Generally, though, the teacher with the martyr complex alternates between the two in a cycle of self-punishment and helplessness—and either way, they're complaining about it.

The teacher with a martyr complex won't take any initiative toward fixing problems, and when something is solved, they immediately find something wrong with the solution, as well as another problem to complain about.

Every challenge that arises just reinforces their belief that the job is impossibly difficult. Their viewpoint is classically pessimistic: they ignore the positive things that happen and selectively focus all their thoughts and energy on the negative. The teacher with a martyr complex appears to hate their job, but actually thrives off of telling themselves what a saint they are for staying in such a demanding profession.

Both the true martyr and the person with the martyr complex often feel helpless (*"If I don't do it, who will? I can't say no!"*) and fall into the victim role (*"I can't believe I'm the one who has to handle this again— everything would fall apart if I didn't step up."*)

People who hold these mindsets are often physically sick and worn down, which reinforces their victim mentality and seems to legitimize their claims of self-sacrifice.

> **The true martyr honestly believes they cannot stop doing everything they're doing; the person with a martyr complex thrives off the drama of *imagining* they cannot stop. Both use work as a diversion and distraction from their real issues.**

Though they say, "The responsibility is totally on me all the time," they actually do not take responsibility for their choices at all. They just mindlessly follow down the same well-worn path, mumbling to themselves that "a teacher's work is never done."

Choosing a more empowered approach

Whether your struggle is with feeling too much responsibility or not accepting enough, this is the choice set before you:

Do you want to feel bad for yourself, or do you want to choose thoughts that feel better?

As Joyce Meyer has said, it's your decision to be pitiful or powerful: you cannot be both. Many times we want to be powerful in front of others, but behind closed doors, we enjoy wallowing in our self-pity.

Here are some ways you can train your mind to embrace a more constructive way of thinking:

1) Choose empowering replacement thoughts. Use the strategies of dismiss, distract, reject, and replace. Tell yourself: *I'm feeling sorry for myself, and that kind of self-pity just isn't helping me feel the way I want to. I am not at fault for everything; neither do I have the power to control everything. But, I CAN control some things. I choose to set my mind on the stuff that's within my control and not keep wallowing in problems I can't do anything about.*

2) Examine the evidence. Challenge your distortions by asking, *"Is this really all my fault? Do I truly have a reason to feel guilty about this outcome?"* or *"Is this really all someone else's fault? Have I played even a small role in the outcome?"* Put your responsibility in the proper context, and figure out what the best course of action will be for the future. Focus on acknowledging your errors honestly but without judgment so you don't get stuck in thoughts that feel bad.

3) Decide when to exercise your right to self-pity. Even though your disempowering thoughts may be true, that doesn't mean they're worth thinking. Maybe your situation IS really bad—a big mistake is completely your fault, or you are totally a victim of someone else's choices. You're allowed to feel sorry for yourself if you want! The question is whether that's actually what you want, and for how long. Observe your thoughts and the reaction they create in your body and moods. Just because you have a right to be upset doesn't mean that exercising that right will be beneficial.

4) Adjust your expectations. This is a topic we'll address in more depth later, because having flexible expectations is absolutely crucial for a healthy mindset. When you encounter obstacles that make your job more difficult, practice not letting yourself totally off the hook (*I can't possibly do my job well with this happening!*) or blaming yourself entirely (*I have to get this done the right way right now or something terrible will happen!*) Use the additional evidence you gathered and view your level of responsibility in the most accurate sense possible: *I can't complete this task as well as I'd like because of the circumstances, but I can still do x, y, and z to the best of my ability.*

5) Practice a sustainable level of energy expenditure. The pressure to be "on" all the time for students is a great contributor to misplaced responsibility issues. Find your personal balance between teacher-led activities and student-directed work so that you're not constantly instructing. Give yourself permission to sit down on occasion. Will your students learn more if you are continually circulating around the room and interacting with them? Maybe. But you can't sustain that behavior for six hours a day, five days a week without exhausting yourself. Of course, that's no reason to swing too far the other way, give up, and sit behind your desk all day long. Figure out which activities are the best use of your energy and give them all you've got—

but don't expect yourself to keep up that effort during every moment of every day. Play around with different class time structures so that you can accommodate your high energy and low energy times without sacrificing instructional quality. Establish balance so that your "on" moments are less energy draining and you can have more of them.

6) Remind yourself that no one is indispensable. The school ran itself before you were there. It will run itself after you are gone. You don't have to do everything. If something doesn't get done, it doesn't get done! If someone else does it and their efforts aren't to your standard, let it be: done is better than perfect. Similarly, you are not dependent on anyone else for your day to run smoothly. Be careful not to let someone else's shortcomings be the reason why you didn't pull *your* weight. Do what you can do, and focus less on everyone else.

7) Refuse to round up other people who will collude with you, and band together instead with educators who have a vision and goals similar to yours. Be aware of which teachers drain your energy and bring out the worst in your personality, and avoid conversations with them on potentially discouraging topics. If you can't resist the urge to complain, tell someone with a positive mindset, "I need to share a problem with you. Don't agree with me that it's a really bad situation. Just let me talk, and afterward help me put things in perspective." Having the support of other educators (in your building, district, or even online) can help you feel less alone in facing the problems that drain your energy. We're stronger together: don't attempt the insurmountable all by yourself.

8) Challenge disempowering messages you hear. Exercise discretion when listening to other people's opinions of what's wrong with schools. Just because someone in a position of authority says something is true does not mean you need to accept it blindly. Teachers are not responsible for all of society's wrongs, but neither are they all innocent, helpless victims of the system. Question anyone who insists otherwise. Accept responsibility for your part but don't take on a bigger burden than you can carry.

9) Separate your work from your results. Always strive to maintain a commitment to the process, rather than basing your enthusiasm on the results you see. Much of your work as an educator will not show an immediate payoff. If you expect to see positive forward progress on a consistent basis and that doesn't happen due to factors beyond your control, you'll feel discouraged. But if your commitment is to The Work, then you'll stay focused on fulfilling *your* role and playing *your* part. You'll be able to feel a sense of satisfaction in your work that is separate from whatever outcomes you can or can't achieve.

10) Advocate for necessary change while centering your own wellbeing. Being upset about an injustice or disservice to children does not actually help the kids. Being sad or angry alone is not activism. These emotions can be the impetus for change, and you can funnel that anger into something productive. But spending your weekends moping around and dwelling on all the problems doesn't fix them; it just drains your energy and creates unhappiness. So, don't be afraid to center joy, health, and wellbeing for yourself. By paying attention to your own needs and ensuring that you're spending time in fulfilling, enjoyable ways, you'll have more energy to advocate for change when you have the opportunity.

Replace anxiety with thoughts that feel better

"Did you hear about the new curriculum we're getting next year? My friend who teaches at Sunset Middle uses it already and says it's so much work! They have to make a ton of copies—like the budget's going to leave us any money for paper—and there's no way we can cover all those skills at that pace. It's totally overwhelming and impossible. She's ready to quit and said we should transfer to another district now before it's implemented at our school."

"Yeah, and on top of that, Mrs. Jones wants to retire soon and who knows what nutjob principal will replace her. If we get somebody like Mr. Krenshaw over at Sunset, we're gonna have to turn in lesson plans every day, and that's gonna be impossible with the new curriculum. I swear, if they increase our class sizes on top of all this

like the Gazette said was going to happen, these kids don't stand a chance. I can't teach like this!"

What a depressing--and yet familiar--conversation, right?

Whether it's venting to one another after dismissal or just random chatter in the lounge during lunch, conversations like these drag you down, steal your peace, and rob you of your joy. Even if you don't participate, just listening can make you feel hopeless.

And the worst part?

It's all for nothing...*because none of those problems actually exist.*

In this present moment, the old curriculum is still in place. There is currently some money for paper and copies. Mrs. Jones is still running the school and hasn't retired. Class sizes are the same as they were in August.

The entire conversation centered on a forecast of anticipated problems.

Fear is useful; anxiety is not

Anxiety, worry, and apprehension are all emotions that crop up when we think about *potential problems* in the future. These emotions are different from the fear we experience when facing problems in the present moment.

Fear can be a very useful emotion because it enables us to respond appropriately to current threats. Our bodies were designed with effective fear responses like fight, flight, freeze, fawn, and flop.

But when we worry about future threats, our bodies' stress levels rise despite the lack of immediate danger. We inadvertently prepare ourselves mentally, emotionally, and physically to respond to the threat, and our levels of the stress hormone cortisol rise.

And because the problem is an imagined future problem, the short-term present moment danger never arrives and our nervous systems can't downregulate. Instead, we're left holding the tension in our minds and bodies with no outlet for it.

Dr. Emily Nagoski and Amelia Nagoski refer to this as a need to "complete the stress cycle" and intentionally practice ways of downregulating when we've experienced stress or trauma.

Otherwise, trying to continually anticipate potential problems will divert energy away from the tasks at hand. We become quickly wrapped up in fabricated problems that are impossible to accurately predict, and when a real-life matter presents itself, we become too distracted and irritable to handle it.

I can't tell you how many times I had to restrain myself from snapping at a student who interrupted me while I was distracted by some future conflict. *Geez, get the knot out of your own shoelace, kid, I'm busy.* I'd want to say. *I'm trying to figure out how to respond to the principal if she tells us we have to come in on Saturday for the PTA meeting. It's a union violation, I tell you! We're going to fight this!*

Anticipating problems is an especially dangerous habit in the field of education, where policies and procedures seem to change on a dime for no apparent reason and against all logic. It's impossible to predict the next demand or circumstantial change.

Mentally preparing is different from worrying

So, why do we expend our mental and emotional energy on something we can't possibly foresee?

People like to anticipate problems because it makes us feel prepared. No one wants to be blindsided by a major change, so rumors fly fast when new developments surface. It's a natural human reaction to think about problems that may arise and start devising coping strategies.

But as I think you've seen throughout the course of this book, our automatic brain response is not always the healthiest one.

Living in the future is just as destructive as living in the past. Anytime we are not fully present in this moment, we're depriving ourselves of experiencing the *now*. We have to consciously set our minds on the present reality, and remind ourselves that the majority of problems we anticipate never happen.

It's absolutely fine and good to give yourself some time to anticipate future problems for the purpose of problem-solving. Weigh a few possible choices you might make and consider how you could respond if various scenarios play out.

This can keep you from feeling completely unprepared if a problem does arise. So if you're worried your beloved principal might retire, think through what might happen if she did:

I would be upset, and there's a chance our next principal could be really bad. If she does retire this summer, I could put in a transfer request to a different school just to give myself another option. But I like my school and my colleagues, and I don't really want to leave. I'll probably just stay and stick it out with a new principal. If it's really bad next year, I can always leave after that. But, I know I'll be fine no matter what. And who knows, the next principal might even be better in certain ways.

This kind of self-talk allows you to think through what might happen in the future without getting sucked into a spiral of anticipated problems. Anytime you start to think about the principal retiring, repeat these replacement thoughts to yourself:

If she retires, I'll be okay. I'm open to whatever comes next. I know that there are more good things happening for me in the future and I don't have to be fearful that everything's going to fall apart. I'm strong and I know I can adapt to new situations.

Then if the principal does announce her retirement, you won't feel so panicky, because you've already thought through your options and reminded yourself that you don't need this particular principal in order for you to be happy and thrive as an educator. You'll likely feel bummed out at the announcement, but not devastated, because you mentally prepared.

Can you see how this practice is different from worrying? It's not about imagining every possible thing that could go wrong; it's about considering some likely outcomes and reminding yourself that none of them are the literal end of the world. Then, if and when they do happen, you won't be blindsided—and you also won't have spent weeks, months, or even years in a state of anxiety waiting for that particular thing to happen.

How can I be okay if this worry comes true?

When I get caught up in worrying about all the possible things that could go wrong, I like to remind myself that there are ultimately just two possible outcomes: something "bad" that I imagined will actually happen to some degree, or it won't.

If a bad thing doesn't happen, I'll be fine.

If a bad thing does happen, I can create a plan of action then.

That's all! This approach really helps me when I'm overcomplicating situations and trying to envision every possible outcome.

I remind myself that it doesn't have to be that complex. Everything will be fine and I'll get through it, or else it won't be fine and I'll discover a way to get through that, too.

Either way, my worrying won't change the outcome (though it could make things worse if I make myself sick from stress.) So, I might as well dismiss the thought from my mind and get back to whatever's happening in the present moment.

If that feels too difficult, I can explore all the ways I can still be alright even if the bad thing happens. I'll listen to the prediction I'm telling myself and ask, *"How can I be okay if this turns out to be true?"*

I can mentally list what I'll still have. For example: *I'll still have my family. I'll still have all my teaching experience. I'll still have all the wisdom and skills I've acquired over the years.*

This puts me in the frame of mind to brainstorm ways I can still be okay if that worry does indeed come to pass:

I can get emotional support from my friends, and won't have to face it alone. I can consider a transfer to the school where my best friend teaches. I could revisit the idea of moving to that other place I've always wanted to live. I can explore the career opportunity my friend told me about. I can find other ways to make money and use my skills.

And, while I'm making decisions, I can use my evenings and weekends to disconnect from school and do things I love. Even if the worst outcome happens in this scenario—we get a new principal and I'm absolutely miserable in my work--I can find ways to still be okay.

If these are the last of the "good old days," enjoy them

It also helps to remind myself that worry will *always* lead to regret. If nothing bad happens, I'll regret having spent my time being anxious for no reason. And if something bad does happen, I'll regret having wasted my last few days of peace and normalcy.

If this is the final glorious year with Mrs. Jones before she retires, shouldn't I be savoring every day that she's still principal? Shouldn't every moment now be that much more precious? Wouldn't I be happier by enjoying the predictability of stable, strong leadership while I actually have it?

The best use of my life is to maintain my joy and wellbeing. If I'm miserable and anxious, then I can't do my best work or show up for the people who need me. I also can't easily enter into a creative state of flow and productive problem solving in order to deal with issues as they arise.

Choosing not to keep worrying about potential problems is a decision I've never regretted. No matter what happens, I know I can look back and think, *Yep, I had the right attitude and the right mindset. I made the most of every day. I don't always know what's going to happen, but I trust that I will be able to find my way through whatever challenges may come later, and I don't have to figure everything out right now.*

Here's an example of how this mindset has played out in my life.

Every spring, one of the biggest stressors for teachers is the possibility of being moved to another grade level or school (and in some cases, being "surplussed" or pink-slipped and having no position at all.)

I've heard rumors about who might be surplussed the following year as early as *November* of the current school year! And throughout May and June, the teacher's lounge is always abuzz with nervous energy and speculation about who's retiring, who's taking leave, who's quitting, and what's going to happen to everyone else.

There were several years when it seemed highly probable that I'd be moved to another grade level due to student population shifts. The first few times that possibility was raised, I freaked out and worried constantly.

As I practiced new ways of thinking, I found myself responding differently. When everyone (and I mean everyone) asked if I was worried, I'd shrug and answer, "Nah. I'll either get moved to fourth grade, or I won't."

They always looked perplexed. "But what if you DO?"

"Then I'll teach fourth grade."

"But...aren't you mad you're going to have to learn a whole new curriculum and move all your stuff to a different room?"

"If I have to, I'll deal with it when I know for sure it's happening. But for right now, I'm still teaching third grade, and that's all I'm thinking about."

This answer was usually met with blank stares. People just didn't know how to respond. They'd either start worrying about their own situation again, or say wistfully, "I wish I could be as laid back about it as you are."

I'd usually laugh at that point, because I'm NOT naturally laid back, and my instinct is to get wound up at the thought of involuntary change. I had simply practiced not anticipating problems, and in the process I'd re-trained my mind.

As it turned out that year, another teacher voluntarily moved to the fourth grade slot and the problem never materialized. I felt a great deal of relief, not because I wasn't changing grades—I had already made peace with that possibility—but because I hadn't stressed myself out for three months over nothing.

What to do when you anticipate problems

If you struggle with worry or anxiety and feel like it's controlling your life, I have some recommended resources for you TruthforTeachers.com/awakened.

But, for general tendencies toward anticipating problems, try this 4 step process:

1) Recognize what you're doing.

Label the thought immediately: *I'm thinking about something that is not a problem in this moment. Everything is fine right now.* Reminding yourself that there is no immediate danger or need to act will de-escalate the situation in your head and ward off the fight-or-flight adrenaline response that comes with panic.

2) Allow yourself time to productively problem solve.

If the issue is really bothering you (or if you have some control over the situation and need to think about your course of action), go for a fifteen-minute walk and allow yourself to think about possible outcomes and *positive* responses. The fresh air and exercise will keep you from getting bogged down in the problem and open your mind to more possibilities. End the walk by repeating (and possibly writing down) the thoughts you've chosen to dwell on.

3) Talk about your concerns openly with just one or two confidants.

You don't need to tell everyone how you're feeling. The more you discuss a source of stress, the more you create a stress response in your body. And if you confide in people with negative mindsets, they will respond in ways that create even more anxiety.

I recommend choosing no more than a handful of people to talk with, and make sure they are in the right mental space to give an encouraging response. I prefer to complete the first two steps before talking to anyone so that I am already calm and in a positive state of mind.

Not only does this keep me from giving voice to endless rambling concerns, it also makes it easier for the other person to be supportive. Many times, I have already gotten over my anxiety by the time I talk to someone else and am just filling them in on a potential concern and my chosen response to it.

Remember, the anticipated problem is occurring in YOUR head. Don't dump everything on a bunch of other people and expect them to fix it.

4)   Choose your replacement thoughts.

If your mind doesn't replay the potential problem, someone will probably ask you about it, so practice your response:

Everything is fine in this moment. When the time comes, I'll have the information I need to make a good decision, so I don't have to think about it now when things are up in the air.

Every time you start anticipating a problem, dismiss the thought immediately and replace it with constructive thinking. Be gentle with yourself, the same way you would with a child or a dear friend who's struggling with anxiety. Give yourself a pep talk:

This is going to be okay. You've got this. I trust you to handle this and make it through.

Replace judgment
with curiosity

One time early in my teaching career, I had a student I'll call Ellen who didn't complete her homework several times in a row.

Not yet having many strategies to help kids who didn't turn in their work, I called her over to my desk and prepared to deliver my standard teacher lecture on The Importance of Being Responsible.

My intention was to scare her with the possibility of a phone call home. (I'd not yet learned what a crapshoot THAT threat is.) With a stern tone I asked, "What do you think your mom would say if I called her right now?"

Ellen blinked expressionlessly. "She told me I didn't have to do my homework because it didn't matter. She said I could go outside and play."

Oh, really? I was taken aback, and fuming inside. This parent was undermining my authority and totally demeaning the importance of education by saying homework didn't matter!

I could barely even look at Ellen that morning because I was so angry. At lunchtime, I ranted about the conversation to my coworkers, which got me even more worked up. This perceived slight had wounded my pride, and I took it out on my students for the rest of the day by being overly harsh and impatient.

I couldn't focus on anything but what I was going to say to that parent when I called. *The nerve of her! As uninvolved as parents at this school are, I should've expected such an unsupportive response. I'm going to teach her a lesson about undermining school policies!*

After students were dismissed for the day, I called Ellen's home and asked to speak to her mother. "I wanted to let you know that Ellen hadn't turned in her homework the last few days, and when I asked her about it, she said you told her homework didn't matter and she could go outside to play."

I paused to gear myself up for whatever might come next.

"That's the story she told you?!" said Ellen's mother incredulously. "What I *said* was, it didn't matter whether she did her homework first or played first. I give my kids the option to go outside and get their energy out right after school if they need to, and then start homework afterward. That's what she opted to do, and she told me she did her homework when she came inside. Her older sister even said she checked it! Are you telling me that Ellen has not only lied about doing her homework, but tried to make me look like I was fine with her not doing it?!"

Well, then.

Turns out I had worked myself up into a frenzy over nothing.

I had taken what Ellen said and immediately assumed it was accurate, which led me to make unfair generalizations and jump to all kinds of conclusions.

That was the day I learned why many teachers tell their students' parents, "If you promise to believe only half of what your child says happens at school, I promise to believe only half of what they say happens at home!"

Four types of presumptuous judgments

Jumping to conclusions means rushing to judgment without having any or all of the facts.

Anytime you presume to know what other people are thinking, feeling, saying, and doing (and feel entitled to make judgments about what you *think* you know), you're working from distorted thinking.

You'll remember part of Dr. David Burns' list of cognitive distortions from the chapter about explaining setbacks in a pessimistic way. Here, I've organized four more of Burn's distortions and their sub-types under the category of making presumptuous judgments:

1) Labeling: Naming what you see without having the evidence to substantiate it

I labeled Ellen's mom as an uncaring parent based on a single piece of second-hand information. I also over-generalized the "uncaring parent" label to apply to *all* parents in the school, using the incident with Ellen's mom to reinforce my belief that most parents at the school were generally unsupportive and uninvolved.

The mental habit of labeling can apply to judgments about other people as well as self-labeling (e.g. *I forgot to assign that project again today—I'm such a forgetful person.*)

Dr. Burns also includes a cognitive distortion he calls "mislabeling" under this category. Mislabeling is describing a person or an event with extreme language that is inaccurate (e.g. *I am such an idiot for forgetting the assignment!*)

No one likes to be labeled, and it's important to take time to gather evidence for our beliefs before boxing people into categories which might be unfair.

2) Mind Reading/Projection: Assuming that your thought system is the same as everyone else's

Let's say you consider not attending a meeting because you think it's a waste of time. You end up dragging yourself there anyway and notice that one of the administrators didn't show up. You might jump to mind-reading conclusions like, *He knew this meeting was stupid and that's why he bailed. Why does he make us go to these dumb things when he doesn't even have the integrity to show up himself?*

Mind reading is a type of presumptuous judgment that can surface without us consciously realizing it. We simply assume that others have the same self-talk and motivations as we do, and base our responses on that false assumption.

A healthy mindset considers other possibilities and gathers more evidence before making judgments. Ask yourself, *"What else might be true that I haven't considered?"*

For example:

Maybe he had another meeting to go to, or maybe he got stuck talking to a parent at dismissal, or had to watch a child whose parent didn't come to pick-up on time. I'll probably find out tomorrow when I drop off the reports to him, and until then, I'm not going to waste my energy wondering about it.

3) Fortune Telling: Assuming your prediction about the future is accurate

This is one of the most dangerous aspects of jumping to conclusions because your negative assumptions can create a self-fulfilling prophecy.

A fortune-telling thought like, *"I don't know how to teach decimals so these kids get it—they're going to bomb the chapter test"* gives you an excuse for doing less than your best, and justifies giving up on students before they have a chance to show what they can do.

Similarly, a thought like, *"This parent conference is going to be disastrous!"* predisposes you to polarizing, catastrophizing, and other tendencies of the pessimistic explanatory style. You've already told yourself things won't go well, and due to confirmation bias, your brain then looks for evidence of this belief. Your mind will be highly attuned to anything negative that happens and will disregard the positive because it doesn't fit your existing judgment.

A more accurate thought that avoids fortune telling might be, *"I don't know how this is going to turn out, but it's not helpful to anticipate problems. I don't have enough evidence to make these assumptions, and can never know in advance if it's going to go well or poorly. So, I'll try to go into this situation in a calm, emotionally neutral stance so I'll be better prepared for whatever might happen."*

4) Emotional Reasoning: Assuming that the way you feel is an accurate reflection of reality

I feel like a bad teacher; therefore, I AM a bad teacher.

I feel like my assistant principal hates me, so he MUST be trying to get me fired.

I feel like this new teaching strategy isn't going to work, so I have no reason to give it a shot.

So many of the assumptions we make from a place of emotional reasoning are based on stories we're telling ourselves. These are conclusions we've jumped to based on the way the situation makes us feel and our own personal interpretation of others' behavior.

Our emotions and personal interpretations aren't inherently a bad thing, but they aren't 100% accurate and therefore have to be interrogated. So, dig a little deeper when you find yourself getting worked up.

What are the facts, and what is the story you've been telling yourself about the facts? What have you been thinking about that contributed to this mood or feeling? Who have you been around that may have influenced your mood or feelings?

Using reasonable assumptions and unpacking bias

Sometimes we have to make some assumptions in order to plan our next course of action. This is typically a problem only when we assume the worst or unfairly characterize a situation and begin obsessing over it.

When Ellen told me that her mom said homework didn't matter, I could have gathered more evidence before drawing any conclusions. A healthier thought pattern would have been, *"Hmmm. This story doesn't sound right. I need to talk with her mom and make sure we're on the same page in terms of homework expectations."*

It could have been that simple! Instead, I was distracted and anxious all day. I kept repeating my assumptions to myself rather than waiting until I had enough evidence to form a valid opinion.

It also would have helped to withhold judgment (and detach emotionally) until I had more information. Even if I had assumed that Ellen's story was completely accurate, I could have avoided harm by not proclaiming a final judgment to myself about the type of parent Ellen's mom was.

Rushing to judgment made me closed off to the possibility that she did in fact care about her daughter's homework, and made it harder for me to accept new information that countered my previous assumption about what was true.

I've always considered myself an intuitive person, and I used to misperceive my habits of labeling, mind reading, fortune telling, and emotional reasoning as part of my intuition. Now I understand that the times when my intuition was "off" occurred because I had fallen into cognitive distortions.

Sometimes these distortions were based on internalized biases, prejudice, and stereotypes that I hadn't examined and unlearned. My gut instinct was telling me something that wasn't true because those biases were ingrained in my thinking and I didn't realize they were there.

Looking back, that was clearly part of the problem in my interaction with Ellen. Because the school I taught in had a reputation for being in a "bad neighborhood," there were a lot of stereotypes that I believed about the families who lived there. I'd heard many of my colleagues complain about how parents were absent from their children's lives and didn't value education.

So, when Ellen said her mom didn't care about homework, I was primed to believe that was true. After all, that was a reasonable conclusion to draw when I hadn't truly interrogated my beliefs about the community I taught in, or developed deep enough relationships to see past what outsiders had told me about it.

I brought in my own racial, cultural, religious, and socio-economic norms, and filtered the situation through that lens. This caused me to assume things were true based on my own background, rather than the realities of the individual humans I was interacting with.

If you often follow your instincts and find that they occasionally lead you astray, pay attention to whether any presumptuous judgment habits (including unexamined bias) are the culprit.

Humility is always key in getting to the truth of a situation. There are so many things that we will never know about other people's lived experiences.

So when I rush to judgment or start making assumptions about the cause of people's behavior, I remind myself, *You don't know everything. You are not inside that person's head. There's no need to form an opinion on every issue, label every action, or make a judgment about every situation. Just relax and observe. Focus on understanding, not on placing people and events into boxes.*

Gathering more evidence and waiting it out

Preventing yourself from jumping to conclusions or rushing to judgment is a matter of asking questions and gathering more evidence before making a decision. When you feel yourself running ahead of the situation and being presumptuous, acknowledge what's happening and take a step back.

Let's say an ordinarily cooperative student is giving you an attitude and refusing to complete work one day. Here are some examples of distorted thinking, along with replacement thoughts which result in gathering more evidence before pronouncing judgment:

Labeling: There's no possible way I can get through to him. He's a stubborn child. I know this kid: once he's completely shut down, he won't respond to anything. This is impossible.

Alternative Interpretation: He's only been acting this way for one class period—yesterday went fine. I need to observe and interact with him more before I get concerned that we have a major issue today.

Mind Reading: It must be because of the divorce. Everyone's talking about how much his parents are fighting these days. This is just great—what am I supposed to do about his parents? I can't help him when the problem is at home!

Alternative Interpretation: He might be upset about his parents divorcing, but it could be something else, and there was probably a trigger just now. I should talk to him after class and get some insights directly from him.

Fortune Telling: He's going to act like that until his mom and dad stop fighting. This is going to be a long, uphill battle. I can't believe I have another noncompliant kid in this class—just what I need.

Alternative Interpretation: That's only one possible outcome—why leap straight to the worst case? It's very normal for a child to have a bad day and not feel like being cooperative. I'll be sensitive to what's happening and supportive so he can pull through this more quickly.

Emotional Reasoning: I just *feel like* this is going to be a major issue for a long time. This kid will end up being a huge behavior problem for the rest of the year—I can feel it in my gut.

Alternative Interpretation: I probably feel like this is a big problem because I've heard so much about his difficult home life. I've projected other teacher's opinions onto him. And, I might be operating on some stereotypes about how boys behave, and how families from his socio-economic background handle divorce. I need to unpack some of these conclusions I've made and see if they're accurate, rather than just going on what I assume to be true.

In addition to gathering more information, you can also choose to simply *wait*. Many of us are anxious to figure out solutions to problems right away, and we forget that simply gathering more information before acting can be helpful.

In our scenario here about the student withdrawing in class, saying nothing to him about being uncooperative can be useful; kids appreciate a "free pass" on occasion and not having to explain themselves in every single instance of questionable behavior.

While you'd definitely want to uncover the root issues and offer appropriate support, timing matters. Forcing kids to talk when they're emotionally shut down doesn't usually yield much insight and only serves to aggravate you both further.

Just as it's wise to let our own low moods pass before making decisions or taking action, it can also be helpful to provide that opportunity to children.

When we try to solve every problem the moment it arises, we can easily jump to conclusions and make inaccurate assumptions because we don't have enough information yet. So, listen, observe, ask questions, and *then* draw reasonable conclusions about the best course of action.

Being open to new interpretations and evidence

Once you've gathered more evidence or waited awhile, be sure to accept all new information that comes your way and readjust your interpretation as needed.

Your conclusion about the disengaged student could end up being something like this:

I talked to him during lunch, and apparently, another child disrespected him in the hallway before class. It sounds like this wasn't the first time they've had a confrontation, and things have been escalating between them. He was really angry, but he seemed to appreciate the advice and resources I shared with him.

While he might be on edge because of his parents' divorce, there was a specific catalyst for this incident, and it WAS something that I could help with. I'll be sure to observe him for the next few days and see if any new info comes to light so I can offer more support.

Incorporating new evidence into our belief systems can be tough, and many folks get stuck on this step. It's tempting to justify or rationalize our original assumptions:

Well, he SAID it was about an argument in the hall, but that was just an excuse. I know his home life makes him extra touchy all the time. Just watch, the same thing will happen again tomorrow! This is all his parent's fault.

Once we've assumed we know the real story and developed a personal attachment to our interpretation, it can be difficult to accept that we were wrong.

Avoiding judgment in the first place is the best solution. When we work from a place of intellectual humility and get genuinely curious about uncovering the truth, it's far easier to root out cognitive distortions and accept new information as it comes.

Replace worry with mental space for problem-solving

Have you seen the meme that says, "A teacher's brain is like a computer with 3,792 tabs open?"

It's true! Most of us try to hold way too many thoughts at one time. Even though we have calendars, alarm notifications, and notes apps on our phones, we still try to keep a lot of information in our heads, pressing our working memory to the max.

Our minds are thinking about everything we've just done, what we're doing right now, what we NEED to be doing right now, what other people are doing, and what needs to be done in the future.

At the same time, we're critiquing, judging, and comparing things to our own standards and others' expectations. We're also taking in countless sensory inputs, such as phone and device noises, music and television in the background, and the sounds of people around us.

In the classroom, this attempt to process so much simultaneous information is magnified because we're also trying to think about every single student's needs at one time. We're monitoring all of their emotions, behavior, academic skills, and more.

It's no wonder we feel like we have no mental bandwidth and are mentally overwhelmed.

In the dominant American culture, there is a certain badge of honor that comes with pushing ourselves to the limits both mentally and physically. We admire people who appear to be "doing it all" and we perceive them as successful and accomplished.

However, our current pace of information flow and stimulus was NOT the norm for most people throughout history. Our minds were never designed to handle the rate of information we typically process. It's been noted that the average American now consumes more information in a day than the average American in 1850 consumed in an entire year.

If it feels like you're responsible for remembering and managing too much…you probably are.

Clearing out a cluttered mind

The sheer volume of our thoughts about information we're processing can clutter up our minds, just like too much stuff can clutter up our homes and classrooms.

This often manifests as issues with executive function, like word retrieval and recall ability. Amongst all the junk you don't need in your mind, it becomes impossible to find what you're looking for, even if it's right within your reach. Whether it's physical or mental clutter, the space is simply too full.

A cluttered mind also prevents us from doing deep thinking and complex work. When your mind is preoccupied with too many small issues, it lacks space to process bigger things that are more important. We don't have the mental bandwidth to grapple with larger societal issues and ideas around justice, legacy, mission, values, and purpose.

It's like a computer freezing up or running slowly with long delays between your tap on the keyboard and the computer's response. That's a typical result of having too many programs running at one time: your computer has a finite amount of memory available and can only handle a certain number of commands at once. The problem isn't solved until you either shut down a number of tasks or restart the entire system.

Our brains work in a similar way. If you're trying to do or think about too many things at once, your response time drags, and you can't handle any of them well. You have to do a mental reset and clear your mind of the extraneous thought processes.

A clear mind is able to respond to problems calmly and with wisdom. It's focused, and not distracted by all the other thoughts clamoring for attention.

When you've cleared your mind, your mood is higher and you perceive lots of different possibilities. Things that seemed impossible before are suddenly easy to understand. This is why it's so important to keep your mind free of as many unnecessary thoughts as possible.

Creating mental space for problem-solving

You might be saying, "I can't possibly put a big problem out of my mind and forget about it! It'll drive me crazy to know that I haven't figured it out or done anything about it."

That may be true, but only because you've trained your mind to behave that way. Sometimes your brain can be like a stubborn child that insists on having its way, convincing you that you MUST respond to it immediately.

But you are not your thoughts. You are the observer of your thoughts. You have no obligation to respond to a thought that lingers around in your mind, no matter how important it might feel.

Having a calm, clutter-free mind is the optimal mindset for solving problems. Sometimes it's best to abandon issues that bother you--just for the moment—trusting that when you return to them, you'll have a fresh perspective and better ideas.

I was once doing instructional coaching work in a school with a principal I'll call Mr. Russo, and he asked me to help him create class schedules. If you have ever tried to do this, you know that it takes a long time to work out various lunch shifts, special classes, teacher prep times, pull-out instruction and special education push-ins, etc. It's difficult to accommodate every need and impossible to make everyone happy.

Mr. Russo and I worked for about two hours on a basic schedule and then found there was a conflict that seemed unavoidable. We talked about it for half an hour. We had five other staff members look at the schedule.

What if we did this? What if we moved that? None of us could find a work-around.

I suggested that we leave the schedule alone and return to it the following day. But the principal refused. "No, I won't be able to sleep until this is done. It's going to bother me. I have to figure this out today."

I gently reminded him that we had several weeks until the new quarter began, and the schedule could easily wait another twelve hours. This did not give him any mental relief from the urgency he was feeling.

I shared the value of setting problems on the mind's "back burner," and mentioned that solutions often come to people when our minds are the clearest, such as when we're driving on an open road, spending time outdoors, or relaxing. What if we let the problem simmer in the back of our minds until the following day, and came back to it fresh?

Mr. Russo agreed that this was probably the best approach, but he just couldn't let the issue go, and insisted on making a final schedule decision that day.

Though he didn't say so, I know he was apprehensive about trying out a different approach to problem solving. He didn't trust that his own inner wisdom and understanding (which were currently buried under worry and too much mental activity) would resurface later on their own.

I felt very empathetic toward him, but I knew that I'd already contributed everything I could for the moment, and my brain simply had no more left to give. "If you want to keep working, go for it," I said. "I'm going to start on something else."

Mr. Russo worked another three hours on the schedule that day. Though he was normally very friendly and kind to everyone in the school, I noticed he had a curt tone toward teachers who interrupted him that day. He was impatient with a student who stopped by to say hello. The entire time he worked, Mr. Russo mumbled under his breath, *"I'm never going to figure this out. It's not going to work. This is not going to happen."*

I could see the toll his stubbornness was taking on him mentally and emotionally, and it was difficult to watch.

Long after the final bell rang, Mr. Russo found a workable solution to the schedule conflict. But rather than feeling relieved, he seemed even more perturbed. He had exhausted himself mentally and was upset that he had accomplished nothing else during the day. All of his other tasks had piled up and now he was worried about how he'd get them done the following day.

To make matters worse, Mr. Russo had to go home and take care of his young daughter, something he normally looked forward to but was now dreading because of the throbbing headache he'd created.

It had been a miserable day and was shaping up to become a miserable evening because he refused to stop and give his mind space to problem solve effectively.

I share Mr. Russo's story because it's so relatable—we've all been there, right? I can't tell you how freeing it's been to learn to trust my ability to return to problems and solve them later when I'm in a higher mood. I know without a doubt that giving my mind time to clear all extraneous thoughts and THEN attempt to problem-solve will result in my best thinking.

Here's how I learned this: I simply took a chance and tested out the theory—once, twice, three times, just to see if it would work. It did, and now it's my gut reaction.

I persist in a task until the point of near frustration, and when I feel my mood starting to shift downward, I drop the problem from my mind. I force myself to do something else even when my mind insists, *No! Just give me five more minutes, I know I can work this out!*

Mounting frustration is a signal that the solution isn't yet in my conscious mind, so there's no need to wrack my brain any longer. I have to clear my thoughts first so that the answer will surface from a deeper, calmer place within.

There are many instances in which a seemingly unsolvable problem actually resolves itself on its own while I wait. But I don't have to depend on that—since I know it's unlikely that the problem will go away on its own, I can actually feel good knowing that it will still be there.

That means I am free to return to it at any time. I can give myself permission to relax and do something else. Often a new idea comes to me within minutes when I'm not even thinking about it.

What percentage of worries are legitimate?

Many people expend a great deal of time and energy worrying; that is, thinking negatively about past and potential concerns. Thoughts of worry are followed almost instantly by feelings of anxiety and concern. Within just a few seconds, worry can create a stress reaction in the body.

Additionally, some people are more prone to worrying than others. Psychologists call these people "ruminators." They're the type of people who tend to play mental reruns of past events, anticipate problems, and analyze things over and over. I have this tendency for sure!

Ruminators worry about things constantly and rehearse various scenarios in order to feel prepared. Ironically, this intense concentration can make it harder to solve problems because it takes the person out of the present moment and overloads their brains with more information than they can hold at one time.

One way to deal with excessive rumination is to examine the evidence for things we're worried about. The late philosopher Earl Nightingale researched what he called "the fog of worry" in our minds, and classified it into five categories:

40%: Problems that never happen
30%: Things in the past
12%: Health-related worries
10%: Petty, miscellaneous concerns
 8%: Legitimate issues

The past cannot be changed. Anxiety about your health can make your condition worse. Petty worries that are only important for a few moments (like whether you'll get a good parking space) are obviously not worth the energy expended. So, 92% of the things we worry about are not worth expending our brainpower on.

A 2019 study published in the journal *Behavior Therapy* largely corroborated Nightingale's conclusions. In their subjects, 85% of worries did not happen. With the 15% that did happen, 79% of subjects said that they discovered they could handle the situation better than anticipated or said they learned something worthwhile from it.

That study's conclusion? 97% of what subjects worried about turned out to be untrue, an exaggeration, or a misperception.

Exact numbers aside, I think it's clear that we spend way more time than necessary worrying about future problems that never actually occur...and that means you can use mental reframing tools to help yourself see the situation from a different, healthier perspective and dismiss, distract, reject, or replace unwanted worries.

Thinking productively about genuine concerns

What about our worries regarding impending events, like how students will score on standardized tests? How can we handle legitimate worries, such as the likelihood of budget cuts causing us to lose our jobs?

First, allow reasonable time to contemplate and plan for justifiable concerns. Don't be afraid to think about things that are actually worth thinking about, because it *is* possible to reflect on a problem without creating feelings of anxiety and worry. Just because you're thinking about something that is potentially stressful doesn't mean you have to experience a stress reaction.

Consider the actionable steps you can take and prepare as best you can now. Make good decisions in the present that are likely to cause things to work in your favor later. That means teaching to the best of your ability, and in the case of test worries, giving your all to prepare students for their assessments. Focus your energy on those steps you can take, and implement them well.

If there's nothing you can do, as in the case with teacher layoffs, continue to focus on what's within your control at this moment: work hard and enjoy the job you have now so that you feel good about what you've accomplished each day. Don't let yourself slowly descend into apathy. Choose thoughts and behaviors that you'll be able to look back on with satisfaction.

Experiment with different ways to reframe the event anytime you're tempted to worry. Tell yourself: *I'm hopeful that my students will do well on the test. I'm also expecting a few surprises and I won't be thrown off balance by them. I've done my best to prepare the kids, and their actual performance is out of my control. I don't have to burden my mind with it, because there is nothing I need to do or figure out. I know that whatever happens on the day test scores come back, life will still go on.*

In the job loss scenario, you can reframe things this way: *I would love to have my position next year, and it would be very difficult if I lost it. But, the situation would not be impossible. Tough, but not unbearable. I can handle whatever happens, and I will ultimately survive and be just fine. I'm trusting that things will work out for my good in the end. I can't control the situation, but I can make it easier or harder on myself depending on how much time I spend thinking about it. I'm choosing to give my all in the classroom each day, and not worry about the future.*

Finding the big picture

Whenever you're tempted to start brooding, distract yourself. Throw yourself into meeting other people's needs. Altruism is only part of the reason why people participate in animal rescues and volunteer at homeless shelters; they also do these things because it makes them feel good! There's just something about helping someone else solve their problems that gives you a broader perspective on your own problems.

If the last thing you need is another obligation on your time and volunteering seems out of the question, focus on meeting the needs of people already placed in your life. Look for opportunities to be helpful toward others in your regular routines. A small favor conducted for someone else can give you a wonderful feeling inside and distract you from your troubles for hours or even longer.

Though meeting your own needs brings pleasure, doing things for other people brings gratification, a feeling that has deeper and more lasting effects. You'll find (as many research studies have confirmed) that your mood stays higher and your life satisfaction level increases when you focus on doing things for other people.

Another perspective besides altruism that may help: consider that there is no prize at the end of life for successfully tackling all the things we worry about.

There is no gold medal for keeping your house clean on a daily basis. There is no eternal reward for making sure you always look presentable at the grocery store. In the grand scheme of life, it will not matter if you checked your children's homework every single night without fail.

So many of the things we get anxious about are not being noticed by other people. They come with no external punishment or reward. What ultimately matters is how we feel when doing them and what they add to our lives.

Are the habits we're striving to establish really the things we want to do?

Do we genuinely care about the accomplishments we're so worried about achieving?

Are the possessions we're preoccupied with acquiring or maintaining truly worthy of that effort?

What concerns are the best and highest use of our precious time and energy on this planet?

Like everything else, letting go of your rumination habits is a process. Over time, you'll become more mindful, letting go of any thoughts about the past or future and continually focusing on what's important in the present moment.

Being aware and appreciative of every small good thing you're experiencing in this moment of your life can become a habit for you. Rather than wishing and worrying, you'll practice embracing happiness, peace, gratitude, and contentment until it becomes your instinctive response. It's a slow but drastic mental shift away from negative thought patterns into ones that enable you to enjoy your life.

15

Replace expectations with radical acceptance

You can envision the entire lesson in your mind: the students are going to LOVE this learning experience! You stayed at school until 5 pm transforming your classroom, then went home and put a few more hours into last-minute material prep. You almost couldn't sleep thinking about how excited the kids would be when they walked into the classroom and saw what you'd prepared.

And then…nine kids were pulled out of class to do make-up testing, and the fire alarm went off before you even had a chance to do the introductory activity. The element of surprise is gone and the "wow effect" is totally ruined.

It's an anti-climactic reward for all of that effort, and you can't help but feel agitated. *This is not how it was supposed to happen! It should have been an awesome introduction to our new unit.*

We've all had experiences--both in and out of the classroom—in which we have high expectations and a clear idea of what we think will happen, only to be whacked in the face by reality.

There's no way to totally eliminate that experience, because it's a natural part of being human. But, we *can* ease the disappointment by noticing when the "shoulds" start popping up, and letting go of rigid preconceptions of how things are supposed to happen.

Openness to other possibilities

Let's be clear—having *some* expectations is a good thing. We establish classroom rules and procedures and expect students to behave appropriately. We schedule meetings and expect others to show up on time. These sort of expectations are reasonable norms, and help us keep systems and processes running smoothly.

The only time our expectations create a problem is when we refuse to accept any other outcome.

Instead of insisting that things "should" function a specific way, be open to other possibilities. You can expect students to behave, but when they don't, accept it and deal with it. Expect your co-workers to be professional, and when they're not, concede that it happened and move on.

This is a much healthier response than clinging to your expectations and repeating them over and over in your mind: *They should not be acting like that! This is unacceptable! Everyone is supposed to do things the right way!*

Holding onto expectations when it's clear they won't happen can create fearfulness and panic. It causes you to live in a constant state of low-grade anxiety as you worry about whether your numerous expectations will be met.

Thinking so much about what you want to happen causes you to identify too closely with the anticipated outcome; you can't let it go because it's a part of you. Any other outcome becomes an attack on your beliefs about how the world should work and who you are as a person. The ultimate result is that you lose the ability to accept any reality except the actualization of what you expected.

If you want to feel more consistently calm and peaceful, examine your expectations and determine whether they serve you or weigh you down. When a particular expectation is only creating frustration and bitterness, you cannot hold on to it.

Staying positive without preconceived expectations

Our natural human instinct to avoid disappointment is very strong, and it can be tempting to think that optimism is the problem: *Maybe if I lower my expectations, I won't be disappointed when things don't go well.*

Expecting the worst then turns into cynicism or pessimism. You begin going into every situation anticipating problems: *This probably won't go well. No one's going to like it. I know this will be a disaster.*

So, be cautious of the habit of lowering your expectations. All it does is trade potential disappointment for guaranteed discouragement, and deprives you of the pleasure of anticipation.

> **To keep a positive attitude without holding on to preconceived notions of how things will go, look forward to an event with optimism, but avoid having any specific expectations. When the event occurs, accept each moment for exactly what it is. In other words, hold your expectations loosely and stay open to different outcomes.**

When you get up in the morning, tell yourself that you're going to have a good day. You're going to choose to be positive and productive regardless of what happens around you. Focus your anticipation on the things that are completely within your control, such as your own attitude and behavior. Don't run down a list of the outcomes you expect from others.

Then, when something happens in a way you don't like, dismiss the urge to mentally compare reality to the way you envisioned it.

If a few kids start spewing four-letter-words at each other during your usually peaceful bell work time, dismiss thoughts like, *Here we go again, I thought this was going to be a good day. It's all going downhill from here.*

Instead, deal with the situation and get yourself right back on track mentally: *Okay, that's handled. I'm proud of myself for not getting heated. I'm going to stay calm and continue to have a great morning with the kids. The day is not ruined. Life is not over. I'm moving on and ready for whatever comes next.*

To do this, you have to be determined to accept reality. The instant you realize things are not happening according to your expectations, resist the urge to compare. Tell yourself, *This isn't the outcome I expected, but it's alright. I'm open to different realities, and I trust that good things can still come out of this.*

If you're a person who likes to be in control and has a hard time letting go, train your mind to believe that the unexpected holds good things.

When an English Language Learner puts together a five-word sentence for the first time, hold that incident in your mind: *Wow, that was amazing! I'm so proud of Mario. It's so exciting to see his progress as he becomes bilingual and masters a second language.*

Conversely, when another child mocks him for mispronouncing one of the words, handle it, and dismiss it from your mind afterward. Don't let the rudeness of that student steal Mario's thunder or drag down the high energy of that moment.

And, don't include that incident when telling all your coworkers about Mario's great progress. Instead, focus on Mario's accomplishments, and stir up those happy feelings in your retelling rather than detracting from it by recalling the part that didn't align with what the experience "should have" been like.

This is a practice of holding tightly to the good part of your day, and holding the bad stuff more loosely. The negative memories become weaker in your mind, because they're overshadowed by the great stuff you keep thinking about over and over.

As you go through the day, be aware of things that add to your joy and dismiss thoughts about things that don't. You're not whitewashing the day and pretending nothing went wrong. You're intentionally recalling the things that went well, instead of all things that you disliked or didn't get done.

Tell yourself, *This really was a good day. Mario had a major development, I wrote all my lesson plans for next week, the class as a whole did really well on the history test, and that hilarious conversation with Kim on the playground was priceless. There were a bunch of things that didn't go according to my expectations, but I have lots of other things to feel satisfied with today.*

Avoiding other people's fear-based expectations

As you start to disconnect your experience of happiness from your expectations about how things "should" go, beware of getting sucked into other people's presumptions and expectations.

For instance, some of your colleagues may have a habit of expecting the worst (catastrophizing) or getting indignant about how they think things are supposed to happen. This can be especially difficult at the start of the school year when you're about to get a new group of students. Your colleagues may bombard you with expectation-laden questions:

"What do you think class sizes will be like this year? Oh, geez, do you think you'll get Manuel or Sammy in your class? Do you think I will? Do you think this group is going to be lower than last year? I've heard they're super far behind, and there's a lot of behavior problems, and I bet this class will be harder."

Don't feed into this type of thinking. Just shrug and say, "No expectations. I'm open to whatever happens." You could even add, "I'm going to make it the best year possible."

You can also channel some of your future-focused mental energy into goal-setting. Creating goals for yourself is a good thing and very different from creating expectations. Goals are things you're working toward; they help you focus on your vision. Be open to many different possibilities as you work toward those goals, and accept each step that comes along the way.

Staying present and open to current experiences

The surest way to ruin a good time is to decide in advance exactly how it's supposed to go. Life becomes much more enjoyable when we're flowing with whatever's happening instead of fighting against it.

Keep your mind focused on what's actually happening, rather than drifting toward what should be happening. Each time you start to imagine what the future will be like, try not to hone in on specific details such as what other people will say and do, what the weather will be like, or what kind of mood you'll be in.

Just hold on to a positive, anticipatory feeling and tell yourself, *This is going to be a worthwhile experience. I'm going to find some good stuff in this situation no matter how it unfolds.*

Hold that good feeling inside of you and bring your mental focus back to the present. This approach opens you up to more possibilities beyond the one you imagined, and trains your mind to be aware of good things as they happen rather than attune to the negative.

I find that when I'm able to be open to other possibilities, the outcome can be better than what I would have planned.

Instead of expecting that friends will be getting together at a quiet, cozy dinner, I can stay open to a different environment: boisterous and stimulating can be fun, too.

Instead of expecting that students will choose a certain book I'm hoping they'll pick for the next read-aloud or novel study, I can be open to their choice: reading a different book can shake things up a little bit and inspire me to try some fresh and interesting things in my lesson plans.

Of course, it can be difficult to resist creating expectations. All of us want to have certain stories to share and memories to hold, and when other people don't behave in ways that fit with those expectations, it's natural to feel some disappointment.

And, it's good to speak up for what you want and need. Let other people know your preferences. Just make sure that you don't have a strong preference for every detail in every situation, or an attachment to those preferences that is so strong, you can't be happy unless things go your way.

This is about noticing adaptive and maladaptive behaviors.

Pay attention to when having expectations creates a happy anticipation, and when it creates anxiety.

Notice when expectations help you feel prepared, and when they create frustration and insistence that things go the way you planned.

Choose to set expectations in a way that serves you well and is healthy for people around you.

Practicing radical acceptance toward yourself

Radical acceptance is a useful approach in our inner dialogue or self-talk when there are certain things about our work — or any aspect of our lives, for that matter — which we cannot change.

Practicing radical acceptance doesn't mean you approve of the problems you're facing or deem other people's inappropriate behavior as okay. You don't have to let people walk all over you, ignore a problem, or tell yourself it's okay that something awful is happening or has happened to you.

It means you stop wasting energy resisting reality. You stop complaining and bemoaning how terrible things are. You need all your strength to teach, and practicing radical acceptance will keep you from draining your energy with perpetual outrage.

Radical acceptance allows you to deal realistically with the facts of the situation (rather than the story you're telling yourself about the facts) and sitting with discomfort instead of insisting something shouldn't be true or isn't really true.

It's being brave enough to see ourselves and accept ourselves exactly as we are. You may not like certain things about yourself, but you can accept that those things are part of the reality of being you. That's different from denying it, being defensive about it, or hating those qualities about yourself.

Even as you let go of behaviors that aren't serving you well, you can accept each stage of that journey. The goal is to see yourself for who you really are, without judgment, and without labels, so that you can work with what you've got.

Many of us are trying to work with an ideal version of ourselves that doesn't actually exist, and we never feel like we measure up.

Others of us are working with the worst possible interpretation of ourselves and feel bad about who we are.

Radical self-acceptance means seeing all of you and accepting all of you. You don't have to love everything about yourself or everything you say and do. You're simply accepting reality rather than fighting it. You're not expending any energy wishing things were different or complaining, judging, or shaming yourself about it.

When you practice accepting yourself exactly as you are, you're able to let go of those thoughts that make it harder for you to be your best. You're no longer working against your own thoughts. Self-acceptance also gives you a model to follow when you need to accept others.

Practicing radical acceptance of other people

Radical acceptance of other people requires accepting who other people are. It's knowing that you cannot change them and it is not your responsibility to do so.

We can influence them, but we cannot control them. We can believe the best about them and believe in their capacity to do better, but we cannot change them. We can only change our thoughts about other people, and how we choose to respond to them.

> **So even when we are in situations where we cannot leave their behavior unaddressed, we still need to approach things with the understanding that we cannot control how other people think, feel, behave, or act. This is part of radical acceptance: seeing others fully for who they are without taking on the responsibility for "fixing" or changing them.**

This is a difficult principle to apply with your students, particularly when you see the potential for greatness in them and sincerely want to help them be their best.

But I promise you will actually have more of a positive impact on them when you practice radical acceptance about who they are because you're able to see them for their true selves instead of giving into beliefs that they should be different somehow.

I want to emphasize that radical acceptance is not a tool that you can realistically expect others in your district to use. You will need to practice radical acceptance about the fact that your supervisors don't practice radical acceptance. Because in a sense, you are being evaluated on how much you *are* able to change your students: by how much they learn, and by how they behave when they're with you.

Learning to practice radical acceptance of your students will keep you from internalizing this pressure, and shift the way you see your role in the classroom. It's a tool to help you resist a toxic system in which you are mentally carrying the responsibility for things that are out of your control.

Just because someone places that weight on you does not mean you have to carry it; just because they say it is your responsibility does not mean that you have to believe it is.

You have influence over your students, not control. This means your choices in the classroom can escalate or deescalate problems. You can make things better for kids or worse.

We want to use radical acceptance as a tool to move us back into a place of empowerment, where we have a healthy and realistic assessment of the situation and can then choose how best to respond.

When you accept the student exactly as they are and the situation exactly as it is, you can then say,

"Here is the reality of what we're dealing with. What thoughts, words, and actions can I choose to make the situation better? When this particular

incident happens again, what response can I choose that will be less frustrating for me and more helpful for the student? I don't like that it's happening and I don't believe the situation is okay. But I accept that it is happening. I accept that this is my reality right now and I am choosing to respond to it constructively instead of insisting that it should not be happening this way."

You can practice radical acceptance toward your students' families, as well. Rather than criticize their parenting skills or the social norms of the community you teach in, practice radical acceptance. It is what it is. Any energy you expend insisting that things "should be" different is wasted. You want to shift from a place of resisting reality to accepting it. Then all that frustration and anxiety can be directed toward something useful to improve the situation.

In practical terms, this is the difference between saying, *"I can't believe parents these days, they just don't care, they should be supporting me instead of ignoring me or criticizing me,"* to saying:

"I accept the reality that my students and their families are living in. I refuse to waste my time mentally replaying how I think things SHOULD be. I'm not going to let my energy be drained away by complaining about their lifestyle or choices. Instead, I'm going to recognize that my thoughts about this situation are creating suffering for me. They make a tough situation even harder.

I'm going to focus on what I can do to help kids get the best outcome possible. I'm directing my frustration toward solutions: I'm looking for ways I can meet their needs in these circumstances rather than blaming them or focusing on how impossible the circumstance is. I'm going to offer support without judgment. What thoughts, words, and actions can I choose that will make things better?"

You cannot change the students who have been assigned to your classroom or their family dynamics. As long as you repeat to yourself, "This kid should not be in my classroom. It's so unfair that I have no support and can't believe I have to deal with this," then you're allowing your energy to be drained away. You are forfeiting your personal power at that moment and fixating on your beliefs about how things "should be."

That's an okay place to go from time to time — we all need to wallow a bit and vent. But you can't stay stuck there. I know from personal experience that many of us, as educators, DO stay stuck there. We complain about the same things every day for the entirety of the school year, worry about and dread those things all summer, and then on the first day back in the next school year, begin anticipating the same problems, waiting for them to happen, and prepare to start complaining again.

Practicing radical acceptance of circumstances

Complaining is an unproductive form of resistance. It's not the same thing as examining a problem from multiple perspectives to understand it better.

There's nothing wrong with talking about inequitable school funding, lack of resources, and systemic problems. In fact, I believe these critical conversations are an important part of radical acceptance. It's very difficult to accept something you don't understand. It's incredibly hard to tell yourself, "This thing I perceive as terrible is happening and I don't know why. It doesn't make any sense, but I choose to accept it."

This is why many of us get stuck in that trap of talking about problems over and over. We're trying to make sense of them. Our brains are pattern-seeking — we naturally want to make connections between different incidents and look for meaning.

I think it's important to work with this natural tendency. When you can begin to make sense of the things that are bothering you by exploring the root problems, it is much easier to practice radical acceptance. You'll find yourself moving from a place of judgment to curiosity.

It's the difference between saying, "I don't understand why things have to be like that," and saying, "What am I not understanding about this situation, and how can I learn more?"

This is particularly useful in our work in schools, given how many of our frustrations center around bureaucracy: testing, paperwork, overemphasis on data, lack of resources, and so on. The better you understand how these systems were created and the way they operate, the more empowered you begin to feel to make a change.

You're no longer helplessly repeating to yourself, "This is so unfair, this is just not right" because you're working to understand the motives of decision-makers, the historic constraints of the system, and the inequalities and biases in the structure of our schools and government.

That knowledge is power. That understanding prevents you from being complicit with the status quo and allows you to instead consciously disrupt it.

In other words, radical acceptance is a principle you can practice to lay the groundwork for productive resistance. Being angry does not create change unless you channel that anger into something productive.

We can take constructive steps to improve working conditions, but do so while practicing radical acceptance of the current reality.

We can change our self-talk from, "I can't believe this is happening," to "It IS happening, and I accept that reality for the purpose of being able to address it in the healthiest, most productive way possible."

So, notice when you are resisting your current reality and creating additional stress, frustration, and suffering for yourself because of it. Just notice when those negative feelings arise and consider the thoughts that precipitated them. Usually when I'm feeling miserable, I've been thinking thoughts like, "This is ridiculous–I should not be having to deal with this."

When you notice those thoughts, it's an opportunity to practice— and I do mean PRACTICE because it takes repetition before it gets easier and more natural—radical acceptance. Practice shifting to thoughts like:

"I can believe it's happening, because it is. This is my reality right now. Not forever, but right now, I accept that this is the situation I'm dealing with and I want to see all the circumstances as clearly as possible. My thoughts that these things shouldn't be happening the way they are, aren't helpful to me. The situation might not be okay with me, and I don't have to approve or condone the situation while practicing radical acceptance. I accept reality rather than resist it. What am I not understanding about this situation, and how can I learn more? What thoughts, words, and actions can I choose that will make things better?"

In the words of Eckhard Tolle, "Accept — then act. Whatever the present moment contains, accept it as if you had chosen it. Always work with it, not against it. This will miraculously transform your whole life."

PART THREE:

CULTIVATING A HEALTHY MINDSET

16

Examine your
unrealistic standards

We've spent some time covering the danger of holding preconceived expectations too tightly, and comparing what *actually* happens to what you *want* to happen.

Now let's take a look at which thoughts these expectations stem from in the first place...and how you can change the benchmark.

This has been one of the most transformative concepts I've encountered for managing stress, and I hope it will make a big difference in your life, too.

Four types of standards

If you find yourself easily irritated by small interruptions and hassles, or notice that you hold onto problems and just can't let go, it's likely due to the standards you hold about what should and shouldn't be happening.

Standards (called "benchmarks" by Dr. Julian Simon) can be divided into four categories:

✓ **Something you feel obligated to do but haven't done:**
  - I should be caught up on my grading.
  - I am supposed to be the kind of teacher my colleague is.
  - I must stop bringing so much work home.

✓ **Something you were accustomed to, but no longer have:**
  - I ought to have smaller class sizes like I used to.
  - I should have the freedom to teach the way I want again.
  - I shouldn't have to test all the time these days.

✓ **Something you're working toward and/or hoping for:**
  - I should be recognized as Teacher of the Year.
  - I have to get an out-of-classroom position right away.
  - I must not have any students score as less than proficient.

✓ **Something you expected but didn't get:**
  - I should have been assigned the gifted class this year.
  - I ought to have gotten a pay raise.
  - I shouldn't have had to stay late for staff development.

I think every educator can relate to at least a few of these sentiments and the feelings of frustration that accompany them. These are examples of how we can create unhappiness by repeatedly dwelling on our standards of how things are supposed to be.

The solution is to identify those thoughts of *should, have to, ought,* and *must* and replace them with less extreme, more accurate beliefs.

Challenging your *musts* and *shoulds*

Think back to a recent lesson in which you were trying to teach, but students were off-task, playing around, and constantly interrupting. Can you remember your self-talk that day?

Maybe you found yourself getting exasperated because you were thinking things like, *These kids are driving me crazy! It's impossible to teach when they're like this! I hate when they act this way!*

Those thoughts stem from certain beliefs about what teaching and learning should be like. Ask yourself, "What standards (*shoulds* and *musts*) are causing me to get aggravated when students are off-task?"

Notice the question doesn't assume that students' *behavior* disturbed you. Their behavior was a contributing factor in your irritation, but it was not that alone—it was also your *beliefs about their behavior* that created feelings of annoyance.

Disruptive student behavior is an inherent challenge to belief systems and benchmarks like:

"Students SHOULD be attentive and respectful 100% of the time!"
"I SHOULDN'T have to deal with any misbehavior!"
"I HAVE to get through this entire lesson today!"
"I MUST NOT be interrupted when I'm teaching!"

Each of these beliefs is relatable, but try examining the evidence for them. *Is it really true* that you should never have to deal with misbehavior, because kids should always be on task? Can you *really know for sure* that this is completely true, or might there be some other way of looking at the situation? Try to challenge your beliefs with more accurate thinking:

"I would like for students to be generally attentive, but no one is on-task 100% of the time (including me.) It's unrealistic to expect an entire class of

kids to all be completely focused during every minute of every lesson. That just isn't the nature of children, or adults."

"I dislike handling behavior issues, but that's part of my job as a teacher. Anyone who works with kids has to help them develop emotional and behavioral regulation. One way I can do that is by modeling it, and regulating my own emotions before responding."

"I would prefer to get through this entire lesson today, but if I don't, it's not the end of the world. The kids aren't machines, and they don't learn according to a strict pre-defined time table."

"I dislike being interrupted, but it's guaranteed to happen sometimes. That's part of life, and certainly part of teaching."

Can you see how each of these statements is more accurate?

Rational thoughts line up with what you experience in the world. Irrational thoughts are based on what you believe the world *should* be like. Frustration occurs when you attempt to make reality conform to your beliefs about it.

Since it's impossible to make everything and everyone conform to your standards, attempting to do so creates frustration and suffering. It's far easier to hold your standards loosely than to control the way everyone around you meets those standards.

This doesn't imply that you should just be satisfied with the status quo and stop striving to make things better. And, it doesn't mean you shouldn't address problems with other people.

Having standards only creates an issue when you refuse to accept things the way they are, and get so caught up in your "supposed to" beliefs that you experience extreme aggravation and anger.

When you *insist* that a certain standard is met and it's not, you can cling to your irrational beliefs and get upset that the world is not operating that way, or you can reframe the situation in your mind.

Reframing irrational beliefs about teaching

See if you recognize any of the following statements from your own thoughts and conversations:

- "I MUST get all my kids to master this content. I can't handle knowing that any of them failed!"
- "I SHOULDN'T have to take work home in the evenings. The amount of overtime in this job is unreasonable and unbearable."
- "I HAVE TO get all the papers on my desk in order right now. I hate leaving my desk a mess. Why am I so disorganized?"
- "I SHOULD BE integrating that app in more lessons. But I just can't keep up with all this new tech! It makes me feel like a terrible teacher."
- "I CANNOT let any student get away with not turning in work. If I don't hold the kids accountable every time, they're going to be irresponsible adults. I can't let any infractions slide and must always be consistent!"
- "I MUST NOT feel unprepared for this parent conference when I'll explain that a child is working below grade level. If I use the wrong words, the parents will think I'm incompetent and stupid. They'll be furious and blame me."

Each of these beliefs sets you up to be stressed when life doesn't work the way you want. Here are some reframed perspectives that are more rational:

- "I WOULD LIKE for all my kids to learn this content, but I can't control that outcome. It would be disappointing if some of them didn't meet proficiency, but it doesn't mean I'm a failure or that they didn't learn anything in my class."

- "I WOULD PREFER not to take work home in the evenings. Realistically, I know it will need to be done sometimes. I don't enjoy it, but I can handle it. My job won't always be fun and completed by 3 p.m. I can set limits on what I'm willing to do at home without being constantly outraged about needing to do it."

- "I DISLIKE having a messy desk, but it's not catastrophic if I occasionally leave work with papers strewn all over. It's okay if I fix them in the morning sometimes. Having a messy desk does not mean I'm ineffective at my job. It will also not prevent me from getting things done in the morning unless I choose to get frustrated about it."

- "I WOULD LIKE to integrate technology more often, mostly because the district requires it. But using a limited amount of technology doesn't make me a 'bad' teacher. I excel in other areas. I'm doing the best I can right now with the time, resources, and knowledge I have."

- "I WOULD PREFER to enforce a consequence every time a student doesn't turn in work, but I don't have to hold myself to that standard. I accept that I will accidentally overlook an incident on occasion, or be too busy to confer with a student about it. There's no reason to believe that my singular oversight will cause kids to become irresponsible adults."

- "I DISLIKE the idea of feeling unprepared in a parent conference. That could make it harder for the parent to understand where I'm coming from. But it wouldn't be horrible or terrible—that's being overdramatic. No one is perfectly articulate all the time, and I can't expect that of myself. Even if the parents give me a hard time, that doesn't shake my knowledge that I'm a good teacher."

What about administration's MUSTs?

In education, we are constantly told there is only one acceptable outcome for us and our students: an extremely high rate of success and/or mastery within ALL tasks and subject areas. Sometimes the standard is 100%—total perfection!

This naturally produces a stress response because it's impossible to live up to that expectation and equally impossible to make our students live up to it.

However, even school mandates can become *preferred* instead of *musts*. You don't have to internalize commands like, "You MUST enter your data by Friday! You MUST demonstrate progress for every student!"

These folks are using extreme language, strict deadlines, and sometimes even threats because they haven't fully developed effective communication and leadership skills. When every directive is phrased as a matter of life or death, resist the tendency to match that sense of urgency and panic.

Evaluate the task from the lens of your own values and priorities, and mentally remove the overdramatic language that makes the demand seem more stressful than it needs to be.

A growing number of administrators are highly conscious of the amount of pressure that "must statements" place on teachers, and do everything in their power to be supportive and not add to the list of urgent demands. But, school leaders are also desperately trying to keep their own heads above water and cope with tons of pressure, which can easily be passed on to teachers.

So, when you're feeling anxious or frustrated, practice translating the request in your mind into something that feels less high-stakes. If inputting data by Friday isn't stressful, then stick with the *musts*. But if you're freaking out because there's no way you'll get it done in time, then reframe the expectation so it's more realistic:

"The superintendent wants me to get my data entered this week. What musts have I created for myself that are actually just preferred tasks? I told myself that I had to change my bulletin boards this week, but that's a preference. I could do it next week if needed. I prefer to get the data inputted on time, so I'll do that instead. Even if I don't get it done on time, it wouldn't be the end of my career. No person follows every single order from their boss exactly when and how the boss wants it. I'm not going to lose my job if the data isn't entered until Monday. This is not an emergency."

Here's another example of reframing urgent directives so the task is put into perspective:

"The reading specialist instructed me to document progress for every single child in reading, but I'm super worried because three of my students are still on the same level as last month. I would like to show evidence of progress. However, I cannot force a child to learn to read faster. I will document everything I can to show that I'm doing my best to meet the kids' needs and that's all I can do. If the reading specialist—who has to examine the entire school's data in her 'free time' between teaching small groups— happens to notice that three children in my class are still on the same reading level, she probably won't even mention it. And if she does, it will not destroy my reputation. I'm quite sure other teachers are in the same predicament with their classes. This is not as horrible as I'm making it out to be."

The idea here is not to devalue the importance of the tasks at hand, but to de-escalate your stress response to them.

This is important because many educators are people-pleasers with high personal standards. We were often excellent students ourselves, and espouse the importance of following the rules and making sure things get done properly. We don't like people to be mad at us, especially when we're trying our best, and we want to be thought of highly by others.

Therefore, we tend to imagine that the consequences for not meeting our own standards (or the ones other people impose on us) are extremely dire.

We live in constant fear of something bad happening because we did not complete our jobs perfectly in every way. A casual request to stop by the principal's office after school fills our hearts with panic as we imagine what we could've possibly done wrong. We allow our minds to imagine all sorts of things that could happen if we don't fill out every form on time, file every paper in its perfect place, and conduct every single lesson with nine types of documented differentiation techniques.

If you struggle with this perfectionism, remind yourself that your standards are irrational and so are your imagined outcomes.

The truth is that your shortcomings usually have far fewer consequences than your mind can dream up. Even with thirty years of experience under your belt, a perfectionistic mindset will ensure that you'll never be able to do everything the way YOU think you ought to.

And yet your students will be none the wiser and continue to thrive! Don't be so hard on yourself that you can't enjoy the job.

Dealing with daily assaults on your standards

You'll notice that the rational counter to irrational standards always uses less extreme language.

When you use words like *horrible, terrible,* and *awful,* you're implying to yourself that the situation is uncommonly bad and should not exist. Though you might in fact think your condition is especially dire, to insist that something must not or should not happen will create suffering.

No matter how obnoxious, annoying, or inconvenient you find a circumstance, it exists! It is happening! And you *can* stand it, because you are!

This is the practice of radical acceptance, and it can help you reframe standards that aren't serving you well. Here are some examples:

Something you feel obligated to do but haven't done:

I feel like I should be the first one to arrive at school in the morning and the last one to leave. I'm always wanting to prove my dedication, and then today I showed up twenty minutes late because I overslept! I'm tempted to be hard on myself about it, but I know I'm holding an unrealistic standard. I don't have to be perfect in order to be effective. I will not lose my job because I was twenty minutes late to school one time. No one even noticed. My principal will not hate me if she finds out.

Even if she was an irrational person and did start treating me differently because of it, I know that I'm a good teacher, and that I'm responsible and reliable. If she or anyone else chooses to hold me to an unrealistic standard, that's their problem! I'm not internalizing their issue. I'm going to focus my energy on doing my job well in this moment.

Something you were accustomed to, but no longer have:

It's hard to accept this new school policy because it doesn't make any sense to me. I keep thinking about how idiotic it seems! But repeatedly thinking about how things used to be better is just a way that I hold onto my unrealistic standard that things should stay the same. "If it ain't broke, don't fix it!" is my perspective. But someone else obviously believed the policy WAS broken. And that's okay. The school system employs people with a wide variety of thought systems and beliefs. Why SHOULD their requirements make sense to me? We're not coming from the same perception of reality.

And, I'm not logical all the time; there's no reason to expect people who create mandates to be logical all the time. Why should I be thrown off guard when we're told to do something that seems senseless to me? I'm going to let go of my standard and accept that policies sometimes change, and not for the better. I don't like it, but I don't have to expend so much energy thinking about it.

Something you're working toward and/or hoping for:

I'm so tired of constantly repeating myself for these kids. Every day, all day long, we practice these routines and procedures so they'll do what they're supposed to do automatically, and they STILL don't have it right! They just aren't at the point I'd like them to be.

Wait—that means I'm comparing their actions to my own standard and upsetting myself when they don't meet it. There's the real problem! People are not perfect. Students are people. Therefore, students will not be perfect. Why SHOULDN'T students misbehave at times? I certainly do! I'm a little bit out-of-control right now!

Something you expected but didn't get:

It seems like everything went wrong today! I just wanted to have a nice, easy day with no major problems. Is that so much to ask? Hmmm. I guess it is. Sounds like an unrealistic standard. I keep asking myself, why is this happening to me? Well, why NOT me? What makes me so special that problems only happen to other people?

Other people sit in traffic. Other people have difficult workloads. Where is the unwritten rule that says my life should be stress-free all the time? There is no law that says things must go right for me, or that other people will never let me down, or that things will not break or fail to work. I need to stop creating rules for life that require things to go smoothly for me so that I'm not inconvenienced.

Tomorrow, I'm not going to base my happiness on whether everyone around me does everything they should. I'm just going to do my part, and not upset myself by repeating all these "supposed to" beliefs in my head.

Stopping the cycle of comparison and evaluation

A major part of contentment is being aware of your personal standards and your tendency to evaluate life accordingly.

The comparison to standards is part of what causes some people in difficult situations to still be happy, and some people in good situations to be miserable.

Dr. Julian Simon calls it your "mood ratio": the comparison between what you perceive your condition to be, and the benchmark or standard you hold for yourself. If you think that your current state compares negatively to your standards, you feel sad.

When you compound that problem with a pessimistic explanatory style, you may assume that you're helpless to improve the situation and things will never get better, which can send you into depression.

Countering your negative perception of reality (by changing your explanatory style and accurately assessing reality) is part of the battle; the other part is challenging your standards. Examine your *shoulds* and where you think you ought to be or how you ought to feel.

You can also increase your happiness level and decrease your stress level by practicing mindfulness. Stop comparing and evaluating all the time and just let things be the way they are. Observe and appreciate what is happening without ruminating on your standards

and expectations. Refocus your mind on the present and handle any
problems as they arise:

*I can enjoy this day without comparing it to other days, or to how I would
have preferred the day to go.*

*I can appreciate this class without comparing these students to kids in my
other classes.*

*I can accept my vice principal for the person that he is and not compare
him to the type of leader I'd prefer him to be.*

*I can do my best with this unit of study and not worry about how well my
colleagues have taught these skills.*

*I can be grateful for the way these events are unfolding, without dwelling
on my idea of how things should be happening.*

Appreciate the principle of separate realities

One day I was teaching a science lesson to my third graders, and made an error with a minor detail. I didn't notice, but one of my students did, and pointed it out with a pretty funny joke that made the entire class laugh, including me.

At lunchtime, I told my colleague what this precocious student had said. "Isn't that hilarious? He's such a cute, witty kid."

My colleague stared at me. "Cute? No, I think it's rude that he corrected you in the middle of your lesson. That's not appropriate. I would have been mad."

We looked at each other in confusion.

Why would that have made me mad? I wondered.

I could see from my colleague's face that she was thinking, *Why would you have thought that was funny?*

It hadn't even occurred to me that this child's behavior might be insulting to someone. I think my perception was probably healthier, because it didn't cause a stress reaction and helped foster the kind of learning environment I wanted. It made me happy that my students didn't view me as a perfect authority figure who could never be questioned, or as someone they needed to fear and couldn't possibly joke around with.

But neither my perception nor my colleague's perception was objectively the "right" or "wrong" way to see things.

We simply have separate realities.

In my reality, it's alright for a child to point out mistakes and share in the teaching process. In my colleague's reality, students should not interrupt lessons by poking fun at the teacher's shortcomings.

Our lived experiences and identities shape how we see the world

The principle of separate realities is why the same student can be a teacher's pet in one class and find themselves getting suspended by another teacher who jumps on that student for every minor infraction.

It's part of why one teacher finds a particular parent overbearing and tyrannical, and the following year's teacher thinks the parent is supportive and helpful.

Separate realities are partially the reason why one teacher might be thrilled at the announcement of a school-wide assembly and another might groan at the thought.

As we explored in the last chapter, whenever people and circumstances don't conform to your standards, you can alleviate frustration by identifying and disputing any unrealistic expectations.

Another major piece to this puzzle (as noted by Richard Carlson) is understanding, appreciating, and allowing for people's separate realities.

All of us see life from within our own frame of reference. Just as you have your own belief system which manifests through your automatic thoughts and self-talk, other people have their own separate belief systems.

No two people's beliefs are exactly alike, because no two people have experienced all the same life events and perceived them in exactly the same way. Our gender, race, ethnicity, culture, religion, family upbringing, education levels, geographic locations, etc. influence not only how other people see us, but how we see the world.

Our interpretation of circumstances is always based on our personal background knowledge and experience—what we already believe is true.

Therefore, since we each have a separate thought system, we each experience a separate reality. These individual realities are shaped not only by our actual experiences, but by our *perception of* these experiences.

This is what makes trauma such a tricky thing: two people can experience identical circumstances, but respond to them in very different ways according to their personalities, background experiences, beliefs, and so on.

A circumstance that might be triggering for one person might not have an impact on another person even if they have some shared background, because no other human has the exact same way of seeing the world.

Sitting with the nuances and complexities of this concept can be difficult. But, doing so can make it much easier to let go of unrealistic standards and truly accept that people think and act differently.

After all, if we each have a separate reality, it's to be expected that we will each perceive and react differently to circumstances, and we'll no longer be shocked when others think and behave so differently from us.

Implicit bias and confirmation bias: why you always seem to be right

The principle of separate realities can help explain why everyone who sees the world differently from us seems to be ignorant, wrong, naïve, or misinformed.

Our perceptions always make sense to us within our own thought system. Beliefs are self-validating—everything we see around us seems to confirm what we already know. Therefore, other people's belief systems conflict with ours because we haven't experienced what they've experienced.

When we learn a piece of information that fits neatly into our existing thought system, we think, *I knew it! I've always been right about this!* That's our confirmation bias kicking in.

But when we encounter something contrary to our thought system, we experience the uncomfortable feeling of holding multiple conflicting thoughts simultaneously. This is called cognitive dissonance.

Our minds think, *What? That doesn't make sense. That can't be true.* We look for ways to toss out whatever information doesn't mesh with our thought system or fit with our "story" about how life works.

Let's say a class is taking a quiz, and one student starts copying answers from another student. The teacher finds out because a third student notices what's happening and tells on them.

How the teacher perceives this situation is based on the teacher's perception of reality.

The teacher might recall the story this way: "It's exactly what I always say—kids these days take the easy way out! They're so dishonest and lazy and have no sense of right or wrong. We are raising a generation without morals! These two kids should fail the class. If this were college, they'd be expelled!"

Another teacher might say, "See, children know in their hearts what's right and what's wrong, and that's why the third child came forward and told me. All three kids knew it was wrong, and now that one of their peers reinforced the need for integrity, they'll think twice before doing it again. Almost everyone has tried cheating at one time or another to see if they could get away with it. It's nothing to get angry about."

Both teachers have articulated the truth *as they see it from within their separate realities*. Neither perception is completely true from an objective sense, because our belief systems are naturally biased.

This kind of bias is often referred to as implicit bias. We may not be consciously holding the bias of "kids are lazy and immoral" or "kids are good at heart." Neither teacher in this situation intentionally chose those views in that moment: it's just how they see the world.

Intention vs impact comes into play here, as it does with any unintentional bias. Both teachers care about justice and want to run their classrooms in a way they believe is fair.

Because of their separate realities, one teacher thinks this requires punishment and a harsh, stern response; the other teacher thinks that the situation requires a model of empathy, conflict resolution, and problem-solving skills.

All people have a right to think from their own unique perspectives. However, all thought systems are NOT equally useful, beneficial, and helpful.

The intention behind both of these belief systems is good, but the impact is not the same. This is why it's so important to examine our belief systems and interrogate our own perception of reality. Good intentions may or may not create a positive impact.

Each teacher in this scenario will probably continue to hold the same viewpoint in the future, because it's difficult to question our thought system when everything happening around us seems to reinforce what we believe.

The next time a child is dishonest, the first teacher will think that's even more evidence that children are routinely untrustworthy and they get away with those behaviors all the time. The second teacher will believe more passionately that the truth will come to light and that learning honesty and integrity is a natural part of growing up. We continually perceive things in a way that reinforces our own thought system.

Examining the usefulness of your thought system

In the previous example about cheating, it's pretty obvious which teacher is more easily aggravated. Is the optimistic teacher's viewpoint more accurate? Not necessarily, but it IS more beneficial. The impact of that teacher's thinking is less stress-inducing and probably contributes more to the kind of class culture the teacher wants to create.

If you find yourself constantly getting upset, you may want to examine your beliefs, self-talk, and thought system and see how well they're serving you. A small shift in your personal perception of reality can make a big difference.

When you disagree with someone, ask yourself, *Who's happier and more at peace? Who's less stressed in this situation?* In trivial issues and minor personality conflicts, it's sometimes better to choose the perspective that makes things easier for yourself.

You could also ask, *What else might be true here? Is there something I could learn from the other person's perspective that would help me see this situation more clearly?* This kind of questioning can be helpful during ideological and worldview differences.

I first began learning the importance of examining my thought system through interactions with my husband. He's far more laid back than I am, and rarely worries or plans ahead.

There have been many times when my stress reaction made me feel like a problem had to be solved right away or something had to be taken care of immediately, and he'd tell me, "Nah, neither of us is in the right state of mind to handle it now. Let's just relax and we'll be better prepared to deal with it tomorrow."

This approach used to infuriate me. I'd wonder, *What does he think we're accomplishing by procrastinating? Why not just get it done and over with? Let's push through the task while we're in a bad mood and be miserable now, and then we can be happy tomorrow!*

I didn't realize I could choose contentment in that moment, and when it came time to handle the problem the following day, I'd be in a better mood and it wouldn't seem so overwhelming.

Eventually, I realized my thought system was not very useful. My husband's outlook was based on a sense of ease and flow, and mine stemmed a lot from anxiety and the need for control.

When I took a more objective look at the impact of our belief systems, it was obviously more beneficial for me to become like my husband than vice versa. Not only did I learn to appreciate his perspective, I began to adapt it myself and nudge my own thought system in a healthier direction.

Being easygoing is not *always* my first reaction now, but the more I practice this habit, the more naturally it becomes a part of my perspective on life—my reality is shifting.

And because it IS important to plan ahead sometimes, my husband has learned to appreciate the way I see the world. In our healthiest moments of communication, we can both step back and interrogate our belief systems: *Whose perspective is going to best prepare us for what needs to get done? Whose perspective is going to help us stay in a calm mental and emotional state?*

Often the answer is: a little bit of both! We do some planning and preparation, but without the agitation of hurrying or pushing ourselves at a pace that feels stressful. In times like these, considering both of our separate realities leads to the best outcome.

Actively appreciating people's separate realities

Separate realities are painfully obvious in our interactions with students. If you've ever caught a child doing something outrageous and baffling, then exclaimed, "Why did you do that?! What were you thinking?!" you know what a pointless question that can be. Usually kids don't have an answer, or can't form a coherent response.

Now you know why! They're operating from a separate reality based on their life experiences and perceptions. They can't articulate it, but somehow, even the most bizarre behaviors make sense in their world.

Accepting this fact means that students' choices will have less power to disturb and frustrate you. You don't have to allow the behavior, of course...but it's helpful to accept that the behavior does make sense within the context of that student's separate reality, identity, and lived experiences.

Appreciating other people's separate realities allows you to be more patient. It's so much easier to be compassionate and not easily offended when you recognize that others' belief systems are just like your own—simply a byproduct of everything that they've experienced and how they make sense of the world.

If you had lived the life they lived, you'd see the world the way they see it. If you'd been exposed to all the information and experiences they have, you'd likely have the same beliefs they do.

When you don't get along with someone or continually disagree with them, it's tempting to blame your differences. But the way you perceive those differences—the story you tell yourself about the differences, and what you make those differences mean—has a major impact on the way you feel.

If we believe that our way is completely right and someone else's way is completely wrong, we can experience a strong urge to convince them they need to change. Sometimes that urge is useful, and at other times it's energy-draining and a waste of time.

Make sure you're being intentional in choosing when you want to challenge someone's belief system (instead of being led into unnecessary or unproductive conflict.)

And, be sure you're intentionally choosing when to let things go (rather than defaulting to your comfort zone and staying silent because it's easier.)

The idea here is to move out of unconscious beliefs and automatic behaviors, and into a space where you're consciously deciding on the best course of action in the moment.

Recognize that your opinions usually come from your own beliefs and separate reality, and not necessarily from unbiased, objective truth. Then you can maintain your opinions without valuing them above your relationships. You can stop trying to make everyone else think like you when you realize their separate reality prevents them from ever doing so.

When you find yourself getting annoyed or defensive during disagreements, you can think to yourself:

- *Everything he's saying is a result of what he's experienced in the world. It's not better or worse than my perception, just different.*

- *There's no possible way she can see the world the way I do, because she has a separate reality. I don't have to get frustrated and think she SHOULD see things my way; if anything, she SHOULD see things differently!*
- *They're not being purposefully ignorant. What they're saying makes sense in the context of all their experiences.*
- *This is how I do it in my reality. That's how they do it in their reality.*

Certainly there are times when other people are incorrect and would benefit from hearing new, factual information. Just make sure you're speaking up in an effort to help people understand different perspectives.

If your intention is to convince others that their viewpoints are wrong and your reality is right, you will likely become upset and experience a stress response, and the other person will simply dig in their heels and become more entrenched in their erroneous beliefs.

Use the principle of separate realities to help you approach students, colleagues, and parents from a place of empathy, intellectual humility, and a genuine desire to understand and connect. As frustrating as other people can be, it can help to remember that they really are living in separate worlds!

Create inner calm before solving problems

By now you've observed how living by irrational standards (*musts* and *shoulds*) and expecting others to view things according to your reality can make life very complicated and unpleasant. When you feel like an experience isn't living up to your expectations or isn't aligned with your beliefs, you may get upset.

You then may *get upset about being upset*...and that's what this chapter will help you address.

Let's say you've spent multiple hours completing report cards the night before they're due. You then discover some reason why you can't submit them (you've left documents at home, you forgot to save or upload digital versions to the server, you signed them in the wrong color ink, used the wrong form, etc.)

If you have unrealistic standards, you might think: *Why did this have to happen to me? This is ridiculous. I can't stand this stupid job! Unbelievable. I should have a secretary like every other professional!*

This initial reaction is pretty understandable, and it's okay to experience that frustration. Ideally, you would be able to let the feelings of anger pass without judging those feelings or holding onto them. You may also be able to regulate your emotions and calm yourself down by reframing the situation.

But sometimes, you're probably going to dwell on those thoughts at length and tell the story of what happened to multiple people. Continually thinking and talking about the problem will keep feeding those negative emotions.

That's the point in which there will be two issues to deal with: the practical problem (your report cards are going to be late) and the emotional response (you're angry and frustrated.)

You may then compound things by getting upset about being upset! You may think, *I shouldn't be so mad about this. It's just a dumb set of report cards. Why do I let myself get so worked up? I shouldn't be feeling this way. This is so bad for my blood pressure! I have to calm down immediately! Why can't I stop getting aggravated?!*

This judgment of your emotional response contains a couple of unrealistic standards. You've convinced yourself that you should never get angry about something relatively minor. And, you've created the expectation that you must stop experiencing a stress reaction immediately. These beliefs only serve to make you more upset because you can't control yourself the way you want to.

How to stop making more problems for yourself

Whenever you upset yourself, you have to deal with both the practical problem (which is the triggering event) *and* your emotional response to it. When you take this a step further and judge yourself for your response (get upset about being upset), you then have three problems.

This is how we wind up feeling anxious about being depressed, feeling angry about being anxious, feeling depressed about being frustrated, and so on. Dr. Michael Edelstein calls these primary and secondary disturbances.

One way through this is to separate your practical and emotional problems. It's generally best to address your emotional reaction first and work backward.

This may feel counterintuitive: after all, if you fix the practical problem, won't that fix the emotional reaction?

However, once you're already worked up, it's generally better to calm down before you attempt to address the practical problem. Otherwise, any setbacks you encounter in solving the practical problem will enrage you more, and make it harder to regulate your emotions afterward because your reaction was so extreme.

So, address the emotional problem first so it doesn't become a greater interference. Simply accept whatever you feel, rather than judging yourself or trying to push the uncomfortable feelings away. Challenge your unrealistic standards that assert you shouldn't have had the emotional reaction you did:

> *I dislike the fact that I got upset, but I accept myself exactly the way I am. I'm not going to upset myself over being upset! Everyone gets angry sometimes. My reaction is in the past and I can't change it. My responses will get more and more healthy as I practice them. Even though my feelings sometimes seem overwhelming, I do have control and I am able to do something about them. I'm not powerless. I do not have to be anxious about being anxious.*

Once you've stopped being so hard on yourself for getting upset, you can deal with the practical problem:

I'm annoyed that I have to redo some of my efforts with these report cards, and it's understandable that I don't want to waste time. But I'm not going to berate myself for making a mistake, or criticize myself for getting upset about my mistake. I don't like that this happened, but it's not "unbelievable" since I do make mistakes on a regular basis. I messed up this time, and it's okay. I CAN stand this job, and I will! I CAN stand to redo part of the work, and I will! There's no universal law that says I won't ever have to do a mundane task twice. I can handle this.

After the secondary disturbances—your emotional responses—are resolved, it's much easier to fix the primary, practical problem. Your head will be clear and your body free from tension, enabling you to problem-solve and make good decisions.

One of the *least* productive things you can do is try to fix the practical problem before tackling the emotional one. Get yourself on firmer emotional ground *first*.

The practical problem will not go away, which can actually be comforting. Know that it will still be there later, and you can handle it when you're feeling better:

I'm not going to figure out the solution to the report card issue right now while I'm still all riled up, and my students are going to walk into the classroom soon. I'll focus on teaching this morning, and then make a decision on the report card issue later during my planning time. I'm still recovering from my initial upset and I'll probably get easily frustrated if the process doesn't go smoothly and quickly. It's better if I do it later, once I've had time to fully accept the situation and mentally move on to other things for awhile. I'll be in a higher mood state later and that will make it easier and quicker to handle.

This process of examining your unrealistic standards and handling any secondary (emotional) disturbances that stem from those standards takes time before it starts to feel natural. Your initial response to minor setbacks may still be irrational and exaggerated.

That's okay, truly. You're human! The occasional yelling of four letter words is understandable. You might not ever be able to eliminate extreme reactions to very stressful situations.

But, you no longer have to let them continue unchecked or feel that you have no control over them. Right after an emotional outburst, you can identify what happened and choose thoughts that feel better.

Talking yourself through problems

Practical Problem	Emotional Response	Judgment of the Emotional Response
My prep (planning) period got cancelled and now I don't have time to prepare for today's lessons.	I feel frazzled and disorganized. I'm panicking trying to figure out how I will get everything done.	I'm upset that I'm feeling so anxious about this. The more I tell myself to calm down, the more overwhelmed I feel! I can't even think about my lessons. All I can focus on is how stressed out I feel.

How can you talk yourself through this situation? The solution is to start with the second emotional problem and work backward.

Give yourself permission to feel the unwanted emotions and show yourself grace even though you didn't react to the practical problem in the way you wished you would have. Next, counter the unrealistic standards and other cognitive distortions that caused you to have the first emotional problem. Finally, once you've calmed yourself down, you'll be ready to deal with the ramifications of the practical problem.

Your self-talk might sound like the following…

Reframe your judgment of the emotional response:

Okay, time to stop and just breathe. I only have two minutes before the kids arrive, and my time is best spent calming down and regrouping. Getting my attitude together is the most important preparation. Whatever paperwork I could do in two minutes won't compare to the positive results I'll get from de-stressing. It's true that I don't have a prep period today, and that threw off all my plans. And it's understandable why this would bother me. I had a lot of things I wanted to get done. No need to be so hard on myself for not being as flexible and easy-going as I would like. At least I am aware that my anxiety isn't a helpful emotion and am trying to be more conscious of it.

Reframe the emotional response:

I feel overwhelmed when I think of everything I need to do. That's because I'm holding myself to an unrealistic standard, and trying to make this day be as smooth and productive as it would've been if I'd had an extra 30 minutes of prep time. That's not going to happen, and it's okay! I don't have to be Super Teacher. I can't magically make up for a half hour of prep time that I lost. This is not the outcome I wanted, but I can deal with it.

Reframe the practical problem:

Now that I've calmed myself down, I can figure out the logistics of not having a prep period today. Let's see: I'll do a simpler lesson with the kids since I don't have time to gather materials. I'll extend the warm-up activity so the class can work independently while I prepare the documents I need. Those phone calls I wanted to make will have to be returned tomorrow. I'd prefer to do it today, but the world will not end if I can't get to it. Okay…I think that's the plan. Let's get this day started and make the best of it.

Here's a final example:

Practical Problem	Emotional Response	Judgment of the Emotional Response
During an important test, one student threw up everywhere and two others got into a fight.	I'm angry that the kids who are fighting disrupted our peaceful learning environment. I'm also upset because I couldn't tend to the sick child due to the fight, and then the whole class got chaotic and I couldn't calm them.	I can't stop thinking about how mad I got earlier. I'm upset that I didn't handle the situation calmly. Why do I let the kids get to me? I'm angry at myself for not acting better under pressure.

This is how you can use positive self-talk to calm yourself down, starting with the emotional problems first:

Reframe the judgment of the emotional response:

I blew it today, but holding everything together just wasn't possible for me in that moment. I was feeling so much pressure because of the test, and when something compromised the test-taking environment, I panicked a bit. I'm being really harsh toward myself, but if another teacher said they'd done what I did, I'd be compassionate and comforting toward them. I'm going to talk to myself as kindly as I would to a colleague: Don't worry, you did the best you could. Next time you'll be prepared for anything!

Reframe the emotional response:

It's pretty understandable why I got mad at the kids who were fighting. I'm taking this test so seriously and they're not! But they weren't the ones who upset me; I upset myself with my "supposed to" thoughts. I couldn't accept the fact that students were fighting when they HAVE TO be quiet and MUST let others take the test. I know these two kids have lots of stuff they're dealing with because they get in fights all the time. It actually makes sense that they WOULD start a fight today, since tension is already running high. They know they don't have a good chance of passing, anyway. When I really step back and look at the whole situation, all of our actions totally made sense within our own separate realities. I don't like the way any of us behaved this morning, but I accept that it happened, and I'm not going to keep thinking about it anymore.

Reframe the practical problem:

Now that I've made peace with the whole morning's events, I'm going to focus on teaching for the rest of the day. During my break, I'll stop by the principal's office to talk to the kids who got in a fight and see if I can help them make sense of this, too. By then, I'll be able to approach them from a calm, caring point of view rather than from a place of resentment and anger. In the morning, I'll talk to the whole class before we start testing again and give them a pep talk so they feel more calm and focused. We'll take this one day at a time, and in the end, it's going to be alright. I'm going to get through it, and it's not going to ruin my entire day.

Let go of the stories you're telling about control

I've noticed that many Type A people are drawn to the profession of teaching, and I counted myself among them in the past.

I relished the freedom to run "my room" my way. Being able to decorate and arrange the learning environment however I chose was so much fun. I treasured my ability to be creative in how I managed the classroom and designed lessons. It brought me a lot of joy to design activities that revolved primarily around my own preferences and ideas about how students learned best.

Therefore, it's fair to say that my job satisfaction—like that of many teachers—was based largely on having as much control as possible over the way I taught.

Note that this is different from valuing autonomy, which all professionals need in order to do their jobs well. We're talking here about control: needing things our own way, and trying to make everything fit our own wants and preferences.

Initially, the main problem with my need for control was that it caused me to take students' misbehavior personally. When they didn't follow the rules I set up or participate appropriately in lessons, I considered it an attack on MY system.

Essentially, I perceived their noncompliance as an affront to who I was as a teacher and as a person. Therefore, my biggest source of frustration as a new teacher was that students (and their parents/caregivers) didn't fall perfectly in step with what I wanted them to do, even though it was obvious to me that I knew best.

With time, I learned to create a more child-centered classroom and increasingly sought and valued input from my students and their families. The educational pendulum swung toward giving kids more ownership over their learning, and that was good for me personally (in addition to the obvious benefit for my students.)

There were suddenly far more resources to help me see myself as the "guide on the side instead of the sage on the stage." I started to view the classroom as *our world* rather than *my world*.

As my beliefs evolved, my perceptions shifted, and students who didn't follow *our* rules were no longer challenging *my* authority; they just needed more support to be successful in meeting our agreed-upon class norms.

When I relinquished the need for control, I found that it was much easier to stay calm and not let my moods be impacted as deeply by unpleasant student behaviors or parent conflicts.

But just when I'd started to make strong progress in this area, the state and district began ramping up standardized testing pressures to a level none of us had ever experienced. New and seemingly impossible standards were hoisted on us with one piece of signed legislation.

And suddenly, I had lost even more of my autonomy (or, as we phrased it at the time, the ability to "shut the door and teach.")

This put me on the defensive once again. Anytime a new mandate was issued, I viewed it as an encroachment on my personal freedom in the classroom. I saw the standardization of benchmarks and assessments as a method to control my teaching, which was just fine the way it was, thank you very much.

It's true that excessive testing has a negative impact on both teachers and kids, and interferes with the amount of professional decision-making authority that teachers should have in their classrooms. We can—and should—push back against this in organized and collaborative ways.

However, trying to single-handedly combat bureaucracy by constantly worrying and complaining about it only makes us miserable. Frustration is bound to surface when we focus more on the mandates we're powerless to change than on our response to the mandates, which we *can* regulate.

In other words, the system can be problematic AND our reaction to the system can be problematic. Both things can be true. So, we can examine and improve systems as well as our response to working within those systems.

We can work to create institutional change while simultaneously prioritizing our own mental health and wellbeing. Activism is not incompatible with individual wellbeing, but an excessive need for control definitely is.

When we feel responsible for controlling students' behavior and work habits, the classroom environment, and the way parents/ caregivers and other faculty behave, we are destined to be miserable. Other people will rarely meet our ideals, and trying to force them to do so will feel like a full-time job in itself. Who has time for real teaching and learning when there's micromanaging to be done?

To break free of this habit, it's necessary to identify and root out irrational beliefs and unrealistic standards. There are five common control-related perceptions that steal our peace:

- I need people to know the "right" way to do things
- I need to identify all problems and fix them immediately
- I need to make everything go according to my plans
- I need everything to be fair and make sense
- I need to know what's going to happen next

Those unrealistic standards can be replaced with the following productive thoughts, which are fundamental to a healthy mindset:

- I can accept other people's ways and methodologies
- I can let go of the interpretation that something's wrong
- I can be happy when things don't go my way
- I can handle things that don't make sense
- I can be okay with not knowing

Let's go through each of these replacements for unrealistic standards one by one.

I can accept other people's ways and methodologies

I was once contracted for instructional coaching at a school that did not require teachers to keep lesson plan records. The faculty just followed the pre-packaged curriculum and taught whatever the teacher's manual told them to, rather than using state standards, grade level expectations, etc. to drive their instruction.

I was astounded that the school allowed a for-profit curriculum company to determine what their students learned and at what pace with no deviation. At the time, I'd never seen anything like it.

When I came home from work that day, I was still preoccupied with the situation, and my husband asked what was on my mind.

"It's this new school I started today—teachers aren't required to keep any lesson plan documents! I asked to see one of their plan books and they had no idea what I was talking about!"

He listened carefully before replying. "Keeping a lesson planner that's based on state standards...is that the *only* way to teach? Has every teacher in every classroom throughout time taught like that?"

"Well, no, but that's how we do things nowadays! We *need* curriculum maps and pacing guides to make sure the kids are taught everything they need to know!"

"Did you have those documents when you first started teaching?"

"No..."

"And weren't *you* an effective teacher?"

"Yeah, but I wrote lesson plans with clear objectives!"

He thought for a moment. "Are any of these people effective teachers despite not having plan books? Are their kids learning? Are there still good things happening in that school?"

I was forced to admit he had a point. I'd observed in several classrooms, and the school definitely had some outstanding teachers.

In fact, one of them had the most innovative teaching style I'd ever had the privilege of witnessing—watching her in action was absolutely captivating. (Even now, many years later, her approach and skills still stand out in my mind.) Obviously she knew what was developmentally appropriate for her students and understood grade level expectations well enough that there was no need for her to write lesson plans.

Talk about cognitive dissonance!

Though I couldn't wrap my mind completely around that paradox, I *was* able to return to my belief that there is more than one effective way to teach and plan for teaching. I had lost sight of that belief because I couldn't envision coaching teachers without lesson plans.

I'd fallen into the trap of thinking I couldn't possibly do my job well without certain basic supports in place, just as I'd done so many times before as a teacher.

After that reality check, I decided not to focus my energy on overhauling the way the school had been run for the last sixty years. I was contracted for a very short period of time and decided that my energy was better spent on modeling best practices and helping teachers incorporate them into their instruction.

Through this approach, I stepped back from my place of judgment. Though I didn't *like* the school's strategy and still felt it was important to have lesson plans documented, I *accepted* the situation exactly the way it was.

As I supported the faculty in using different types of technology and hands-on activities, the teachers saw a difference in the way their students learned. I focused on what they needed, rather than trying to force them to operate the way I believed was best.

A few weeks later, a teacher approached me after a professional development session I'd conducted for the staff. He said, "You know, it would be nice to have a way to keep track of all these new strategies and when I'm going to implement each one. Do you think I should keep lesson plans like you mentioned that one time? Could you help me set some up, like a template or something?"

That experience taught me a powerful lesson about the difference it makes when we respect other people's approaches and give them space to draw their own conclusions.

In our educational system, it's far too easy to believe that there's only one correct way of doing things, and that we must force it into existence. This is part of the culture of standardization: the pressure for everyone to be doing the same thing the same way

at the same time, instead of being responsive to the individual humans who are part of the system.

It's always a struggle to balance nudging people and policies toward positive change and practicing radical acceptance of how things are in the present moment. However, I'm convinced this is the path to productive change without burning out.

No matter how much energy you expend on improving your school, it's imperative to embrace whatever stage things are currently at. Appreciate separate realities as well as the process of growth. For me, this has been one of the most essential keys to success as an instructional coach, and I believe it applies equally to classroom teaching.

I can let go of the interpretation that something's wrong

We have the choice in every situation to interpret it as stressful or not stressful. You can make it easier to select the less stressful perception by training yourself not to see potential setbacks as problems.

Let's say you have an important skill you need to teach students today in preparation for an activity later in the week. You're crunched for time but it's critical that you get through the entire lesson in one period.

Fifteen minutes in, someone comes to your door and says they need to pull your entire class, five students at a time, to do hearing and vision screenings in the hallway.

Though your first instinct might be to groan and wonder how you're supposed to teach with constant interruptions, you can let go of the interpretation that something is wrong. Tell yourself:

> *Okay, this is a change of plans, but it's not problematic. These screenings are important, too. And, it will actually be easier to individualize with a smaller class of kids. I can be flexible. I'll use this class period to have the kids work collaboratively in groups of 5 so that an entire group of students leaves together and comes back together, and the rest aren't disrupted. I'll shorten the final activity of the period to make up for the fact that each group is going to miss a couple minutes of the collaborative activity. It's not ideal, but it'll be fine.*

The alternative is to choose the interpretation that this is a major inconvenience. You can sigh at the person doing the screenings, even though this isn't their fault, and feel your heart start pounding with indignation as you think about how administration doesn't respect your instructional time. You can then forge ahead with your lesson as planned, regardless of the fact that students will miss part of it, causing more problems when you do the upcoming activity and the kids feel totally lost.

It all depends on whether you create a story in your mind that there's a problem. You can choose the interpretation that there's nothing majorly wrong, and simply let the situation unfold with the knowledge that you are free to adapt.

This approach can be extremely valuable in all sorts of work-related scenarios:

- *This year I have nine kids with special needs in one general education class! But I'm not going to choose the interpretation that this is an impossible situation. The more we get to know and understand each other, the better things will go. It's a waste of energy to rant about how this is the wrong placement for them, especially since we haven't met and I don't know their abilities or class dynamic yet. I can advocate for these kids and get the support we need, but they're in my class as of now, and I don't want to bring any negative energy around them. They don't deserve that. I've handled other challenges before and I know I can handle this.*

- *One of my students is so far behind the others. I can choose the interpretation that there's something wrong: he MUST catch up, and being behind is disastrous! Or I can choose the interpretation that this student and I are both doing the best we can under the circumstances. He's missed a lot of classes, and that fact can't be undone. And developmentally, I think he just needs more time for mastery. I'll do my best to monitor his improvement and support him, but I won't stress out. This is just reality, and catastrophizing it doesn't change anything.*

- *I've already explained the assignment three times and I still have students asking me if they have any homework and what the assignment is. I can choose the interpretation that there's a problem (they weren't listening, they don't care) or I can choose the interpretation that this is not a big deal. Students don't always listen or remember things. That's a fact of life and not necessarily something I have to work to fix. It's certainly nothing to stress over. I provide as much support as I can to minimize these occurrences, and that's the only time I need to think about it. It's not a problem for me!*

Note that letting go of the interpretation that something's wrong does not require you to ignore your own needs or gaslight yourself into believing everything's fine when it's not.

This is simply one tool in your thought-work toolbox that you can pull out when it's helpful. If something is truly bothering you, it's your choice whether to address it or let it go. You can decide when to speak up, and when not to.

You always have the option to release the interpretation that something's wrong when you want to feel better about the situation and not expend too much time and energy on it. If you feel like your thoughts about the situation are not serving you well, you can let them go and choose another set of thoughts instead.

I can be happy when things don't go my way

Trying to make the world conform to our preferences requires a tremendous amount of energy, so it's important to be intentional about which battles are worth fighting.

You *could* try to coerce everyone in your household to manage chores to your exact standard.

You *could* sternly correct your students every single time they forget to write their names on their papers.

You *could* complain to your team members about a task so often that they just take care of it for you.

But if you've ever done these things (or had someone do them to you), you'll recognize that it's a tough bargain. Eventually, people grow tired of always giving in or being reprimanded, and relationships suffer.

Perhaps more fundamentally, the controlling person has to be constantly on guard, and always thinking about how they can manipulate the people and circumstances around them to make sure things go the way they want.

It's good to work toward positive change, of course, and you don't need to pretend that an issue doesn't matter to you when it does. This is about acknowledging that the issue isn't *all-important.*

> **Though you'd *like* to have things go your way, they don't *have* to, and if they don't, you will be okay. You're training yourself to believe that it's not**

essential for you to have your way in order to maintain your peace.

Take a look at your standards. You might be reinforcing irrational beliefs like: *My classroom MUST be spotless at all times. Students MUST test silently without making a sound. Parents MUST sign and return forms on time.*

Each of these beliefs is an unrealistic expectation that comes from a need for control. Life just doesn't work that perfectly all the time.

Try to train yourself to be more easy-going and less attached to expectations by incorporating positive self-talk:

The kids have made a mess in the classroom, so we'll review clean-up routines tomorrow—I don't have to dwell on it or get upset. I'm not going to let some paper scraps on the floor ruin my good mood.

It's too noisy for me personally when students work in groups, but they're learning a lot, so I can set aside my personal preferences and be content. I'm glad that the kids are enjoying themselves, and it's great that they're practicing collaboration skills.

Parents and caregivers who don't return forms in a timely matter create extra work for me, but my happiness isn't based on their responsiveness. I can still keep a good attitude when things don't go my way. Everyone's late and forgetful sometimes, even me.

I can handle things that don't make sense

It was disconcerting for me to realize that being good at teaching is not necessarily a requirement to be successful in the field of education.

Individuals who possess little or no instructional expertise can somehow land extremely powerful positions. And for those who are in the classroom, being an effective *instructor* is only a small part of being an effective *teacher.*

There are political games that must be played. There are interpersonal protocols to follow and administrative pet peeves to avoid. There are things to document in ways that defy common sense and basic reasoning.

What makes this so baffling and infuriating is that we're constantly reminded of how altruistic our motivations are supposed to be. Teachers are repeatedly told, *It's all about the kids! We're all here for the kids!* The implication is that we're on the same team, and if we each put the kids first, things will work out great for everyone.

After working in the school system for awhile, we often discover that this is patently untrue. No wonder we get frustrated and disillusioned.

The truth is, the unwritten rules in teaching aren't always that different from those in corporate jobs. Like every employee, part of our role is to make our bosses look good. We also have to do certain tasks to please our "clients" (students and families.) Additionally, we have to make things appear a certain way on paper, and make other things happen in practice.

This is not fun. It is not fair. Often our students suffer the most. But upsetting yourself about these things changes nothing. Getting mad is a reaction, not a solution.

Many teachers resent having to "play the game." Author Robert Leahy suggests that the key is to stop viewing it as game playing. Think of it as a strategic approach to being successful in your school and/or district. Dealing with unfairness is part of the job; it's not a personal affront to you, and you are not the only one affected.

Practice letting nonsensical demands roll right off your back; comply with them as needed but don't brood and complain incessantly. Train yourself to see favoritism and inconsistent expectations as part of working in almost any job. Be patient with bureaucratic limitations and misplaced priorities.

None of these things are right or acceptable, but thinking about how bad they are is not helpful. If you constantly focus your attention on bureaucracy, you'll get frustrated and burn out. Keep your mind centered on your students' needs and not on all the behind-the-scenes stuff that wears you down.

This is radical acceptance; anything else requires you to carry the mental load of resisting reality.

It's like getting mad about high gas prices or a long line in the grocery store. If you stubbornly insist, "No! I do not accept this! I will not make peace with this!" you're causing yourself more suffering. In addition to the practical problem, you've created an emotional response which you need to regulate.

So, mentally detach from the situation, and return to the goal of maintaining healthy thoughts and an enthusiasm for teaching. Keep your mind set on thoughts that help you feel empowered:

I will not take things personally, I will not frustrate myself by trying to control things I cannot control. I accept that sometimes things are unfair and do not make sense. I refuse to lose my peace over something inane.

Only when we reach a place of radical acceptance can we work to create change. We have to come to terms mentally with what's happening in order to make it better.

If you really want to shield your students from the inequities and absurdities of the educational system, enter your classroom each day with laser focus on the kids. Don't let bureaucracy preoccupy you to the point that you're too discouraged to do your best for students.

I can be okay with not knowing

The unknown can be a scary thing.

Educators wonder if they'll have a job next year, if they'll have the same teaching assignment, and if they'll get a pay raise or a pay freeze.

Many teachers spend a great deal of time contemplating and talking about the possibility of getting a new curriculum, having increased class sizes, or losing a colleague who's quitting.

We know that anticipating problems is a destructive habit that can be broken. But cultivating the frame of mind in which the unknown is no longer frightening? That's next level self-development.

You will never be happy as long as you insist on understanding everything that's happening and what's going to happen in the future. There will always be something to try to figure out.

So, you can spend time mulling over every possible situation and outcome, or you can choose to trust that when the time comes, you'll be able to handle whatever comes your way.

Often we can calm ourselves down by working out a plausible solution to problems, and convincing ourselves that's how things will go. We feel more at peace because we *think* we know how things will turn out. But the outcome we envision is rarely what happens. It's a mind game we play with ourselves. We become attached to our expectations of how things are "supposed to" go and are then disappointed with any other outcome.

What would happen if we made peace with NOT knowing?

What if we believed that things would ultimately work together for our good?

What if we trusted that our inner wisdom would surface when needed, and we would know what to do when the time comes?

It's true sometimes that ignorance is bliss. I used to search out all the latest gossip in school, listening to every rumor about future mandates and trying to find out everything that higher-ups were doing.

I thought that having more information would make me better prepared for whatever the future held. The more I was in-the-know, the less likely I was to be blindsided by problems, and the more understanding I'd have about how the school and district *really* operated. I assumed that I was protecting and preparing myself.

With time I realized this was faulty thinking. Hearing about problems that did not directly affect me and that I had no power to solve was usually demoralizing. The conversation would end up as cruel gossip or pointless complaining and then I'd feel guilty or uncomfortable afterward.

Sometimes my so-called facts would make it hard to view or treat someone the same way as before. I'd find myself worrying about other people's issues at random times and passing judgment on them. Then I'd waste my energy wondering if the rumors about funding and class sizes and staffing were really true.

The advantages of having the inside scoop rarely outweighed the disadvantages, and after a while, I just didn't want to be burdened with unnecessary problems anymore. "Not my circus; not my monkeys" is a traditional Polish saying that comes to mind.

I think this mindset comes more naturally with age and experience. As the years pass, situations have to be more extreme to faze you and get you worked up. You've seen and experienced a lot, and know the value of not inserting yourself in every problem or giving your energy to everyone who wants it.

If someone starts to share a rumor with me and then bites their tongue, I no longer cajole them into going against their better judgment. "You're right, you don't need to tell me," I'll say instead.

When someone asks, "Did you hear the latest about...?" I sometimes reply, "Don't tell me; I don't think I want to know."

They'll usually laugh but I'll insist, "No, I'm serious. That sounds like it's going to make me mad and I don't need anything else to be upset about."

Though I still feel curious and even a bit nosy about what's going on sometimes, wisdom tells me that I probably don't need to know about most situations. There will usually be little benefit in uncovering someone's faults or mistakes, or learning about a problem that's potentially coming down the pike.

If and when I need to know, I trust that I'll find out from a reputable source, and I'll handle it then.

Not knowing can be a good thing, a real blessing in disguise. We often envy children for being worry-free and oblivious to all the issues we face as adults. But we rarely have as many troubles as we think we do. We bring extraneous problems on ourselves by trying to figure out stuff that doesn't concern us or predict things we can't possibly know about the future.

You don't need to know everything that's yet to come. Focus your energy on making peace with the unknown instead of trying to control it. Tell yourself that not knowing is often to your benefit. Even though you don't know right now what will happen or how you'll respond in the future, trust that you *will* know.

Generate a positive sentiment override

Imagine this scenario: a student named Joe is failing your class and despite the fact that it's almost November, his mother has no idea.

Mom missed your Open House event and the first round of parent conferences. She's signed the interim reports you sent home but made no comment on the fact that you clearly stated he has an F average.

You've tried calling home but the number is disconnected. You've emailed two reminders about the conference you scheduled for this morning, and arrived early to make sure you could accommodate her.

She never shows up, never calls, never sends a note. When you ask Joe what happened, he shrugs.

What's your immediate interpretation of this exchange? It's quite easy to assume that this parent is irresponsible and doesn't care about her child's education.

But what if Joe's mom doesn't read English and is just signing because she's supposed to (or signing what Joe assures her is a very positive report)?

What if Joe's mom is in the third trimester of a difficult pregnancy and can barely get out of bed, much less manage a household?

What if she's in the process of moving, in a domestic violence shelter, caregiving for an elderly family member, or working multiple jobs?

There are any number of possibilities besides "this parent doesn't care." As teachers, we can't begin to comprehend the complexity of all of our students' families and their home lives.

You can probably think of similarly maddening situations you've witnessed in your own classroom. Oftentimes, those families probably had valid reasons for behaving in ways we tend to view as irresponsible.

And many times, those families probably did not. They were being selfish, or lazy, or yes—irresponsible. After all, they're human, and all of us can exhibit those behaviors and traits at times.

It's always important to work to understand family situations and have an open door for communication, of course. But the parent's actual motive or circumstance is far less important than your perception of it.

You don't *need* to know the real story; you need to examine the story you're telling yourself about what's happening.

Automatically assuming the worst is damaging to the parent-teacher relationship and (consciously or not) affects the way you treat the child. Choosing the negative conclusion also damages *you.*

When we get in these self-righteousness headspaces, we create a stress response in the body. As soon as someone asks how our day was, we immediately key in to the most emotionally-charged event, and replay the entire incident, getting ourselves all worked up again.

"Oh, *my* day? I tried to meet with Joe's mom this morning, and you'll never believe it—she didn't show up again!" And now you've found yourself in a demoralizing cycle of vicious judgment and complaining.

An alternative to judgment is curiosity; an alternative to assuming the worst is choosing to believe the best.

The fight against cynicism

Cynicism can be defined as believing the worst about people and their motives. A cynical perspective comes from a combination of distorted thought processes, such as jumping to conclusions, mind reading, over-generalizing, and expecting others to live up to your unrealistic standards and adhere to your perception of reality.

So if you've found yourself exhibiting a cynical attitude and aren't sure how to change it, take an honest look at your mental habits.

> **Believing the best is always a *choice*. It may or may not come naturally, and it's one of many possible interpretations that might pass through your mind. Make a conscious decision to choose that perspective amongst all the others.**

For example, instead of thinking, *The teacher across the hall, Mrs. Roberts, always shows movies in class—she is so lazy and incompetent,* consider the outcome if you choose to think, *It seems like Mrs. Roberts has been showing movies a lot. I know when I've done that, it was because I*

*wasn't feeling 100% and just didn't have the energy to teach. Maybe she's
exhausted, sick, in pain, or overwhelmed by something in her personal life.*

Mrs. Roberts might in fact be a lousy teacher. But what purpose does it
serve for you to think (or worse yet, *say*) that? What good comes from
jumping to that conclusion?

Positive thoughts are energy boosting; negative thoughts are energy
draining. If you're ultimately looking for happiness and good results in
your life, why would you choose to dwell on thoughts that you know
won't produce anything positive?

People always have a reason for behaving the way they do, and
everyone benefits when you choose to respond with empathy. A co-
worker who appears uncaring is almost always acting that way because
of severely distorted thinking and/or devastating life circumstances.
How can we possibly presume to know a person's mind and heart
simply because we teach in a classroom four doors down?

Trust but verify

Maybe you're concerned that other people will take advantage of
you if you give them the benefit of the doubt. But believing the best
doesn't mean being purposefully ignorant.

It's about recognizing both the subjectivity of the situation and
your own inability to be omniscient, and choosing a perception that
benefits you and everyone around you.

My father always taught me to "trust but verify." By that he meant
believe the best and trust what other people tell you, but take the time
to verify their claims as needed.

If a parent known to be honest sends you a note that his child will
miss a week of school so she can have her tonsils removed, trust that's
the real reason. When rumors circulate that the family is in Disney
World, you don't have to stress; just verify the situation when you

inform the parent that the school requires a doctor's note for an extended absence.

If the parent fails to produce a note and the child returns to school wearing a Mickey Mouse shirt, don't allow yourself to get bitter! Remember, there's no sense in carrying around resentment—*you* are the primary beneficiary of letting it go. Choose to believe the best about the family's intentions by mentally reframing the situation:

The fact that this dad lied shows he probably knew it was irresponsible to have his daughter miss a week of school for vacation when she's working below grade level. I'm glad he understood that this was breaking school policy, and I guess I can feel some relief that he didn't flaunt it in my face.

I bet he also wanted her to be able to complete make-up work, which can only be done for an excused absence, not a vacation. So, he probably wasn't lying because he thought I was too stupid to know better or because he doesn't think education is important.

I can understand wanting to take a vacation when it's cheap instead of during Spring Break. In a way, I'm glad the family had some time to enjoy each other's company and create memories. School isn't the only thing that's important—their family time matters, too.

The parent knows I'm aware he lied since there was no doctor's note, but I'm not going to treat his child differently, gossip about what they did, or allow myself to get all self-righteous. I have no control over their family's choice, only my own response to it.

Believing the best is important with students, too. If a child (who has not previously lied) tells you she didn't complete a project because her brother was rushed to the emergency room the night before, show concern and empathy as if the story is completely true.

Then write a note for the parent that says, "Kylie shared that her brother was admitted to the hospital last night. I hope he feels better soon—let me know if there is anything I can do."

That's a *trust but verify* method that assumes the best (as opposed to a cynical note which might read, "Kylie didn't do her project and blamed it on her brother going to the emergency room. Is that true?")

Sometimes a little more discretion is needed with students, since young children have a hard time discerning between fact and imagination and older students become adept at working the system. If a student has a history of lying to you, the relationship is damaged and there might need to be some verification *before* trust.

But in general, choosing to believe the best about students will give you more internal peace and foster stronger relationships. A cynical perspective is equally valid, but not equally beneficial.

Is it naïve to believe the best?

We've clarified that believing the best isn't being purposefully ignorant. It also doesn't mean believing that everything around you will magically get better.

If you tell yourself that your team leader will stop being so condescending and parents will start checking their kids' homework every night, you might be setting yourself up for serious disappointment.

Psychologists who study happiness and human emotions have found that unbridled hopefulness can actually backfire; if you keep believing something will happen and it never does, you can become depressed.

The key is not to base your happiness on what's going on around you. Don't place your hope in some person or circumstance improving. Instead, believe that even if nothing around you gets better, *you* will continue to thrive.

Make the decision that ultimately, you are not going to get burned out by expecting the worst, continually looking for wrongdoing and offense, making negative predictions, and assuming you know people's motives.

You are going to choose to believe the best, because it helps you keep a positive mindset and maintain your enthusiasm to teach. You're making the conscious decision to have an outlook that prevents stress reactions in your body.

Developing a positive sentiment override

Another way to think about this is from a psychological standpoint known as *sentiment override.*

When you hold a positive sentiment override toward a person, they can do something that's potentially annoying or offensive and you won't be bothered. You'll just explain the behavior away ("Oh, it's no big deal, they're just having a bad day. They're not usually like that.")

When you hold a negative sentiment override, you'll harp on anything negative and discount the positive ("Yeah, they did do something nice this one time, but what about the other three million times they were an insensitive jerk?")

You can have a positive or negative sentiment override toward individual persons, groups of people, situations, places, and so on.

> **Your sentiment override is essentially your overall opinion on something and whether you're inclined to view it in a positive or negative light. It works like a filter so you only see things that fit your thought system and personal reality. Your sentiment literally overrides the facts.**

Filtering out all the good stuff is part of the cognitive distortion called catastrophizing that we discussed earlier.

The opposite of this habit is believing the best and choosing to develop a positive sentiment override. This can subdue irritability, raise your tolerance for frustration, and increase the level of patience you feel in stressful situations.

Imagine that you have a student named Shawn who has refused to complete their class work for the fifth time this month. They simply put their head down and won't even try.

If you have a positive sentiment override toward Shawn or toward your students in general, you might be inclined to think, *No child WANTS to get in trouble all the time for not getting their work done. There has to be a reason. I need to talk with Shawn to see if there's anything I'm doing to contribute to their attitude and find out how I can help.*

A negative sentiment override would predispose you to being critical: *Shawn doesn't take this class seriously. They have no respect for me or my rules. I'm going to embarrass them in front of the class—maybe then they'll realize they need to shape up.*

Notice that the objective facts are the same for both thought processes: Shawn is not completing their work consistently. But your perception of that behavior is based largely on your sentiment override, and the outcome of your response will be drastically different depending on which sentiment you hold.

If you respond to Shawn from a positive sentiment override, you're far more likely to build a healthy, trusting relationship with them and your other students. In addition, you'll find that you feel less discouragement and aggravation.

Do you "have it out" for certain students?

Train yourself to pay close attention to your sentiment overrides, especially when dealing with children. Teachers tend to get fed up with dealing with the same misbehaviors over and over, and become anxious to catch and punish certain kids.

We tend to anticipate problems, and are just waiting for students to slip into familiar patterns of behavior so we can pounce on them.

Children sense the negative sentiment toward them, and can find breaking free of it so difficult that they stop trying. If the teacher only notices what's wrong, why should the child try to do anything right?

When your student Jakob insults a fellow student yet again, it's very easy to slip into a negative sentiment override, jump to conclusions, and assume the worst: *This kid is a horrible person and no one can get through to him. I hope one day some kid gives him a black eye so he'll learn not to mess with people. Until then, I'm writing a referral—let him sit in internal suspension for a few days, and see how he likes that.*

Discontentment in this scenario is valid. The child's actions are unquestionably wrong. But punishing out of anger will make it very difficult for you to give the child a fresh start the following day. It will influence your sentiment override and solidify your belief that he's a bad kid.

So, as soon as you notice yourself choosing the worst explanation, choose a reframing that gives you better results:

Something inside Jakob is still causing him to act out that way. He could be seeking attention, he could be repeating what he's heard from someone else, or he could have unresolved anger. My job as his teacher isn't to judge him but to help him. I'm going to choose a response that I think will get to the root of the problem and prevent this from happening again. What good does it do either of us for me to get mad about his issues? I want to care about Jakob and be kind and empathetic toward him, so I have to choose thoughts that create those feelings.

Believing the best means letting your positive sentiment override enable you to overlook (or at least, resist overemphasizing) faults and flaws. This

habit allows you to see past what's not ideal so that shortcomings don't influence how you think and feel about something or someone overall.

Start paying attention to your bad moods and notice whether a negative sentiment override is the catalyst.

Do you feel a shudder or an eye twitch coming on every time you see a particular student? Do you dread attending meetings and walk in prepared to mentally list all the reasons why they're pointless? Do you get a sinking feeling when you see a particular caregiver and automatically gear up for a confrontation?

These unwanted feelings are often the result of negative sentiment overrides. So, practice believing the best:

It's a new day, and I'm going to treat all my students with kindness and respect.

I'm going to listen for something constructive during our lunch meeting and walk away with at least one new tip or idea.

I'm going to smile as I approach each caregiver at dismissal, and make a conscious effort to understand and appreciate their separate realities.

Choosing to believe the best about students, parents, colleagues, and administrators will make you a happier, more effective teacher. Whether you describe this process as refraining from judgment, showing grace, being compassionate, or training yourself to rely on positive sentiment overrides, it's a crucial habit to establish.

21

Choose your own peace over defensiveness

I once had a district supervisor conduct a classroom walk-through during my lunch time—*surprise!!*—to look for school-wide evidence of science inquiry teaching. (Don't ask: I have no idea who she was, what she was doing, or why she choose that time block.)

The kids happened to be eating in the classroom with me that day and watching a district-approved movie. Our visitor was surprised they weren't in the cafeteria.

I exclaimed loudly, "These students completed every one of their test prep homework assignments for the ENTIRE week, so they get to spend their Friday lunch block eating with me in the room!"

I beamed. The kids beamed.

The administrator, with a broad fake grin and an over-enthusiastic tone that dripped with sarcasm, replied slowly, "Woooowww! You guys are *soooo* lucky! You get rewarded for doing what you're already SUPPOSED to do!"

The kids' smiles faltered. Their eyes shifted over to me.

The first thought that popped into my head was, *Excuse me, Ms. Science Bureaucrat, I literally wrote the book on classroom management. Are you questioning how I reward my students? I got 26 kids to complete all their district-mandated homework for an entire week—accurately, I might add—and they're PROUD.*

I gave up my lunch break to reinforce their efforts and show them that I value the time and effort they spent practicing their skills at home. How dare you undermine what's working for students you've observed for less than fifteen seconds?

My second, wiser thought was that I didn't need to defend what I knew was working for my students, and I certainly wasn't going to do it in front of the class.

I kept the upbeat expression on my face. "They're hard workers," I said, smiling at my students. "They *earned* it, and I'm proud of them."

She smiled hesitantly and then changed the subject to my science teaching. I was helpful and accommodating. Then she left the room and (according to the principal) reported back positively about the things happening in our school.

That was the end of her visit...and as far as I know, the end of her impact on our teaching.

After dismissal that day, I debated whether to tell anyone what happened since I didn't want to get stuck in a complaining/ranting cycle. But I realized I hadn't let her offend me, and sharing the story wasn't going to disrupt my positive mood.

"Guess what happened during the walk-through." I laughed as I shared the story with my grade level team. "Of all the things for her to nitpick about. I was so caught off guard! You gotta love walk-throughs from district 'experts'."

My colleagues were stunned, and most of them were furious. "I can't believe you aren't mad. I would have given her a piece of my mind! Why didn't you put her in her place?!"

I shrugged. "If it was our principal, sure, I'd address it. But why bother? I don't have to prove anything to her, especially with all my students listening to our entire conversation. This was sprung on us last minute and no one even knows who she is. She was supposed to be there to assess science inquiry evidence, so for me, it's just not worth getting upset about."

This was an intentional choice, of course: my initial reaction was rage. But I'd quickly weighed my options, and decided I wasn't willing to lose my peace over someone who had no influence on my life and whom I would probably never see again.

It wasn't the case that this person's behavior was acceptable to me. I was simply picking my battles. My principal was happy with how my classroom was running, and so were my students and their families. This stranger's opinion didn't matter.

I have a finite amount of energy to expend each day on foolishness and had already hit my limit. So, I just chose not to give any more energy to that situation and mentally moved on with my day.

Choosing to be offended steals our joy

Pride is like a landmine in the middle of our joy, waiting for some offense or some perceived slight to detonate the explosion.

Our potential for happiness is often littered with prideful land mines which are difficult for others to avoid because they're unpredictably hidden. As soon as someone steps on one, the peaceful landscape is destroyed, sometimes irreparably.

The solution is to search out and disarm those prideful triggers— your unrealistic standards and irrational beliefs.

Let's be clear: you do have the right to stand up for yourself. Being assertive is having the confidence to voice how you think and feel, and that's a healthy response.

But don't forfeit your peace of mind simply because you have the *right* to defend yourself. Weigh the costs carefully when you're tempted to teach other people a lesson about being offensive. Be certain you're facing a situation in which people *need* to be made aware that their behavior is harmful, and plan for a constructive conversation.

Also be careful not to assume the responsibility of "telling people about themselves." Don't rehearse their wrong-doings over and over in your mind, or repeat their faults to others. Don't lay awake at night imagining the confrontation.

If you choose to address the person, do so in the most optimal time and place when they're likely to be receptive, and then let it go. As we tell our students, you are responsible only for YOU. Don't carry the burden of "fixing" everyone else.

Dealing with offense without *taking* offense

Dr. David Burns has an excellent recommendation for avoiding defensiveness. He explains that we should remind ourselves that the critical or seemingly misguided person is trying to express something that is both important and correct on some level. According to Dr. Burns,

> **The most effective response is to try to hear the part that is true without getting upset over the part that is not.**

Our tendency is to get hung up on the other person's distorted thoughts and irrational beliefs, but if we can look past that to the heart of the matter which is grounded in truth, we can help the other person perceive things more accurately *and* strengthen our interpersonal relationships.

Remember the incident I mentioned in chapter 13, where a parent screamed at me for not helping to open her child's milk? As I began to write this chapter, I thought about that incident and wondered what the element of truth was in her words.

I realized for the first time that the only reason she even knew the incident happened was because *her daughter told her about it!*

On some level, the child must have felt frustrated that she'd needed help and I'd refused, and it bothered her enough to tell her mom. Naturally, the mom was upset that her daughter felt a bit neglected.

I probably needed to re-emphasize to my preschoolers that I truly wished I could assist each one of them individually, but I needed their help in making sure everyone's needs were met. In this mom's separate reality, her daughter may have been feeling unsupported, so she addressed that in a way that made sense to her.

How about the truth in the district supervisor's snide comment about my students being so lucky for being rewarded? She IS correct that sometimes students are given bribes or prizes for things that they should do without expecting a reward. Some kids won't lift a finger without asking, "What do I get if I do it?"

In the supervisor's separate reality, that was probably the case with my reward for something as routine as homework completion—I was teaching my students they should work for a reward, not for intrinsic reasons.

In my reality, students needed an incentive to do the additional, boring test prep homework the district had mandated, and deserved something special for putting forth consistent effort over the course of an entire week.

The point here is not about who is right and who is wrong: that's a reductive, overly-simplified approach that keeps me feeling defensive.

Rather, it's the practice of trying to hear the part that's true without getting upset over the part that's not.

Practice withholding judgment to protect your peace

When I'm tempted to get defensive, I try to think back on the ways I've treated other people. Normally I didn't intend to upset them but was simply insensitive or ignorant, and I believe those who mistreat me function basically the same way.

I appreciate the grace other people give me when I'm accidentally rude or put my foot in my mouth. I'm so relieved when I say, "I'm sorry, that came out wrong; I hope that wasn't hurtful," and they reply, "Oh, not at all, I understood exactly what you meant!"

I have surrounded myself with people who rarely take offense, and I can't tell you how much easier that has made my life. I know I can speak freely and honestly with those I am close to, and I want them to feel the same way. I want to be known as a person with thick skin, a person who cuts other people slack, a person who responds with grace.

This includes the moments in which folks "call me in" or "call me out." I want others to trust that I'm not going to immediately get mad or defensive when they tell me I've done something harmful. I'm generally going to attempt to hear the part that's true and understand the other person's perspective, rather than try to make them look wrong so I can look right.

That's an especially important practice when the offense stems from a long history or pattern of wrongdoing. When a person has experienced a lifetime of abuse, racism, misogyny, homophobia, or other trauma, a seemingly small incident can trigger a huge reaction.

Because trauma is stored in the body, a person who's thinking healthy thoughts can find their flight-or-fight response triggered instantly by something that fits a pattern of wrongdoing they've experienced.

It's important for us to be mindful of this when other people get offended by things we say and do. In this kind of situation, it's less about being offended and more about experiencing pain. The goal isn't really to avoid offending people; the goal is to avoid harming them.

Though we didn't intend to cause pain, if another person is feeling hurt by something we've said or done, the appropriate response is to acknowledge that pain with empathy and care. Don't diminish it, justify it, or explain it away.

And when the situation is reversed and we find our own trauma triggered by someone else's actions, that becomes an opportunity for us to heal.

Notice when your reaction seems to be outsized--the person made one facial expression or said one simple thing and suddenly you're raging. It's probably not about that one person or that one incident: your body remembers all the previous times you've felt that way, and all your previous pain is resurfacing in that moment.

Bring your awareness to your body when this is happening, and breathe through it. Sit with the discomfort and feel your feelings, trusting that they will pass!

You don't have to react to the other person right away. Take a few moments to calm yourself, and then decide how you want to respond.

Even when another person is way out of line or has malicious intent, our ultimate goal is always to maintain our own healthy thinking. Don't let someone else's rudeness, ignorance, or cluelessness keep you from being happy.

You are not punishing *them* by being insulted. Each time you think of what a person said or did to you, you're watering that seed of negativity inside your mind.

For your own sake, not theirs, you can choose to counter your conditioned response of immediately taking offense, and instead, practice withholding judgment.

This is another example of radical acceptance: you don't have to approve of what they say and do, but you can accept the reality that this is their behavior and personality. This is what you're working with, like it or not! Then choose your response based on your acceptance of reality—not on how they "should be."

Practice reframing when you're feeling defensive

If you're a touchy person whose feelings are easily hurt, then it's equally important to focus on unconditional acceptance of *yourself.* Sometimes we're triggered because part of what's said touches our deepest insecurities and fears about ourselves.

For example, I had a stranger on the internet write a comment saying that I don't really care about teachers and kids. That was annoying to read, but my primary response was bafflement. It didn't make sense to me. It didn't fit with what I know about myself, and it didn't fit with what people I respect say about my work.

It was much easier to let *that* insult slide off my back than the one from a commenter who said she'd never read any of my books and wasn't interested in my advice because I'm not currently in the classroom. That hurt, because it triggered an insecurity in me—*what if I am out of touch?*

I believe there ARE too many non-classroom practitioners telling teachers how to do their jobs (instead of amplifying   teachers' expertise) and I don't want to be a part of that problem. So when folks leverage *that* kind of criticism at me, it tends to cut deeper.

More recently, though, I've noticed that particular accusation doesn't hurt quite as much. I can only conclude it's because I've made peace with what I do for a living. I know I'd never have the time or energy to support teachers the way I do if I were in the classroom right now. And, I know I run my business with integrity, pay the folks who work with me very well, and use my income to support causes that make the world a better place.

Frankly, I love my job supporting teachers, and the people who think I should go back into the classroom aren't going to pay my bills, run my business, write my books, or produce my podcast for me if I do that. They have opinions about what I should and should not do, but no investment in my daily life.

If I were to quit everything else and go back to teaching full time, those folks wouldn't even notice or care. They're strangers on the internet! And because I'm no longer as insecure about that issue, their words have far less power over me.

Here are some positive replacement thoughts you can choose to think when you are on the verge of getting defensive:

- *I don't have to agree with everyone. This person is entitled to their opinion and it's based on their separate reality, which is totally legitimate. We can agree to disagree.*

- *This isn't worth getting angry over, and I'm not going to make myself upset by thinking about it.*

- *There's always an element of truth in criticism, no matter how ridiculous it seems to me. I'm going to try to uncover and acknowledge it, rather than rushing to defend myself. If I can't find the element of truth, I can ask clarifying questions and use active listening techniques to try to figure out where the other person is coming from.*

- *I see the element of truth in this person's words. Though there's a lot of distorted thinking mixed in there, I'm wise enough to see through it and not get caught up in the potentially offensive stuff. I'm going to acknowledge the part that is legitimate and not worry myself over the rest.*

- *I've certainly said stupid and insulting things in the past. It caused a huge problem when someone got offended instead of believing the best about my intentions. I don't want to treat someone else like that.*

- *I've done something similarly insensitive before, and other people responded with grace. What a relief it would be for the other person in this situation—and ultimately for me—to cut them a little slack instead of getting worked up!*

- *I refuse to get upset. I am a person who is difficult to offend.*

Learning and communicating about your triggers

My encouragement to you is to be aware of situations that easily upset you, and accept that about yourself so that you can be better prepared. If you don't know what upsets you, or you seem to get upset indiscriminately, start noticing your triggers. Pay attention to patterns and similar incidents that make you angry or hurt.

Your triggers may come from past trauma, or being part of a marginalized community and experiencing discrimination. Or, your triggers may come from your own insecurities (which often derive from those traumatic lived experiences.)

When you know what type of situations cause you to immediately go on the offense, you can communicate those triggers to the people close to you, and they can offer extra support. You may get to know what sets off your close colleagues, and be transparent with them about what sets you off.

I also recommend practicing this in your personal life. In a calm moment, tell your partner, spouse, or best friend about your triggers and what they can do to help de-escalate the situation rather than make it worse. Learn their triggers and what they need from you when they're getting worked up.

For example, one of my husband's triggers is being rushed when we're getting ready to leave. If I try to hurry him along, he senses my impatience and gets agitated in return.

We battled over this for years, until we eventually had the self-awareness to articulate our own needs and what we needed from one another. We talked about the situation in moments when we were getting along (not when we were frustrated with each other) and I explained that I hate rushing, too. That's why I bug him about leaving the house on time—so we *don't* have to rush or get stressed out if we hit traffic or the subway train's delayed. I explained that being late triggers my anxiety, and it puts me in a much better mood when he's ready early.

Our process now is to agree in advance about what time we will both be ready to leave, and we are each then responsible for being ready at that time.

If he doesn't seem to be getting ready when I think he should, I might say, "We said 6:15, right?" to make sure we're on the same page and he's aware of the time. He'll say, "Yep, I'll be ready by then," and I trust him to keep his word, staying patient if he needs a couple extra minutes (as I often do, too.) Agreeing in advance on the time we're planning to leave means we can both get ready on our own time table.

When you are aware of your own triggers and communicate them clearly, you no longer have the sole responsibility for handling stressful situations. You can say to the people around you, "This is one of my things; I have a hard time with this. I start to feel ___ when ___ happens. Would you be willing to ___?"

Enlist the people closest to you in helping you maintain your peace instead of getting defensive or worked up. Talk about how you want to feel and how you want to respond in stressful situations, so other people can encourage you to have those reactions and celebrate you when you're showing growth.

Release resentment
and long-held grudges

There are some instances in which it seems impossible NOT to take offense. Sometimes other people do things that are so demeaning or insulting that your relationship seems irreparably damaged.

How do you move forward in those instances? Can—and should—you really forgive and forget?

The consequence of not forgiving fully

I get along with just about everyone, and I'm a hard working person who usually goes above and beyond what's required. My administrators always thought very highly of me.

So when it became clear that one particular principal disliked me, I had no idea what to do.

It started when a co-worker sent an innocuous message to our entire staff using her district email account. It included a link to my website and read simply, "Check out Angela's site—it's fantastic!"

My principal, who was new to the job and paranoid about district oversight, called me down to his office.

"I saw the email about your site. You have religious content on there. That's not appropriate to be shared via school email."

(At the time, I had one main teaching website and a separate blog I wrote with devotionals for Christian teachers. Apparently my principal had visited my main website, and noticed the link to the Christian resources.)

He handed me some district list of separation of church and state requirements. "You need to give every staff member a written apology that your site was shared via a district email account, and explain that your site is in no way affiliated with the school. Please print this apology on your own paper with your own printer and ink, not the school's. I want it in every staff member's mailbox—even for the custodians and cafeteria staff—within twenty-four hours. I won't write you up this time, provided it doesn't happen again."

I was stunned. After all, I had not written or initiated the email, and it was only sent to the teachers, not the whole staff.

In disbelief, I told some colleagues what had happened. Everyone who heard the story—and at the rate gossip spreads in schools, you know it made the rounds quickly—agreed that the principal had completely overstepped his bounds and faulted me for something I had not done.

If the incident had happened to someone else, I might've advised them to tell their principal politely but firmly, "I did not send that email, and I am not responsible for it. What action did I take that I need to apologize for?" Pressing the issue further and getting the union involved would have also been a legitimate response.

However, I chose to do exactly what the principal asked, even printing the apology on my own paper. It felt in my soul like the right decision.

You can probably imagine what happened when my colleagues read that letter: they immediately went to the website to see my "offensive" content!

As the story spread, my website hits went through the roof. Many of my colleagues had no idea I'd created a site to share free teaching resources, and were thrilled to start using the things I'd uploaded and tell other teachers about them.

As I'd anticipated, I came out of that experience looking blameless in the eyes of my colleagues. And, my principal looked like a jerk who didn't appreciate his teachers' willingness to share resources.

I wish I could tell you that everything was fine from then on. After all, I'd done what I believed was the right thing to do, and had followed my principal's instructions. I recognized that things worked out in my favor and was grateful for that.

But unfortunately, both my mindset and my heart attitude were wrong. I was still bitter.

Just seeing my principal made me cringe. I couldn't stand to be in the same room with him, and had to physically restrain myself from rolling my eyes whenever he talked.

Every additional directive that he sent out—don't use student's names in an email, never hang graded student work on the wall, never write any comments on report cards or progress reports—started a whole new round of whining.

This guy micromanages us in constant fear of offending someone, and he could care less that he already offended one of his best teachers! What planet is he on?

I considered transferring to another school, which fortunately was an option at that time. I wanted to be as far away from that man as possible.

And yet, I didn't have an inner peace about leaving. My intuition was telling me: *you're not done here yet.* Though I didn't know why, I felt that I should stay for one more year, and I did.

During that next year, my principal continued to attack me at every turn. He wrote me up for minor infractions and questioned me on the smallest decisions I made in my classroom.

One day, I was leaning on the fence around the playground while my kids were at recess (we weren't allowed to sit down or talk with any other teachers during recess duty) and he said, "Don't you think you should be standing up straight just in case one of the kids gets hurt and you have to get to them quickly?"

Another time, I stayed after school to give a parent workshop I had volunteered to create and present; though I had given him a copy of the handouts weeks ago, he called my room once the workshop had already started and told me one of the pages was copyrighted for educational use only. A parent workshop, he declared, was not educational use—I'd have to collect the handouts from the parents and rip that page out, then redistribute them in the middle of my workshop.

This was my life under his leadership. I was miserable, always wondering when he would jump on me for something else I had done "wrong."

Many of my colleagues had no problem with him at all, leaving me to question whether I was overreacting or creating a problem where there was none. But he continued to hound me about so many minor things that I knew had to start shifting my perspective or I'd have a breakdown.

Choosing forgiveness

I truly wanted a new way to see things that would help me enjoy my job even with these seemingly impossible circumstances. I simply couldn't go on another day with such bitterness and hatred in my heart…but I didn't know how to let it go when my principal continued to offend me on a regular basis.

There was no miraculous epiphany that erased all of my resentment. But I began *practicing* seeing my principal fully for who he was.

His behavior was indicative of a person who was insecure and unhappy. He was constantly worried about some legal technicality getting him in trouble, and saw my creative, child-centered teaching approach as a threat to the standardization he preferred. It was safer to have teachers who simply did as they were told and followed a script, and I was never going to be that kind of teacher.

I'm not sure if his purpose was to force me to quit or transfer, or if he thought micromanaging me would turn me into the type of teacher he liked. I'd never know for sure, but considering different possibilities helped me see things from his perspective.

I could sense the fear and pain underneath his behavior, and I started feeling a bit sorry for him. He was missing out on his full potential as a leader. He wasn't just a tyrant; he was also a person who wanted to be a successful principal and was disconnected from the things that really mattered.

I knew I had to let go of my bitterness and forgive him—for what he'd already done, and for what he might do in the future—so that I could be happy again.

I wasn't successful every day, but most of the time after that when my principal offended me, I chose to think thoughts of empathy and grace. I actively considered the possible "why" behind the "what."

When my principal did something I perceived as unfair or unreasonable, I thought, *This poor guy. He's struggling to be a good leader and just doesn't have the skills. He needs all the help he can get, so I'm going to forgive him for behaving ignorantly. His choices make sense in his separate reality. I'm not going to let my beliefs about how he should be acting cause me to get upset. I want to enjoy my job. I'm choosing not to give this situation any more of my energy.*

This was hard to do. But I knew my feelings would follow my thoughts. I didn't want to feel anxious and bitter, so I practiced choosing thoughts that created feelings of peace and contentment.

It was a daily battle for the remainder of the school year, but I was able to experience the peace of forgiveness even when the offense was not going away.

Reminding myself that bad situations don't last forever was a great comfort. I told myself constantly, *You will not have to work for this man for the rest of your life. Either he'll move out of your way, or you'll move out of his. No one is going to prevent you from accomplishing everything you're meant to accomplish. He's just not important enough to keep you from doing the work that you're here on this planet to do.*

I woke up one morning in May and knew in my heart that it was time to put in a transfer request for the following school year. I stopped by a co-worker's classroom and asked about a school she used to teach in, since it had a great reputation for caring, supportive administrators.

She emailed her former principal and raved about my teaching, and the principal reached out to schedule an interview with me. There was an opening for the following school year in the same grade level I was currently teaching and loved.

My interview was the following day, and I was hired on the spot— no reference check with my current principal required.

Just like that, in the course of twenty-four hours, I was free from the only principal that ever actively disliked me. It felt like a supernatural intervention or a promotion from the universe: I had passed the "forgiveness test" and was ready for another challenge.

Vindication does not always bring closure

Looking back, I can't imagine my principal had a very good reputation with other school leaders, so it makes sense that my new principal valued the recommendation of her former staff member instead. Also, I think some things are just meant to be, and will fall into place with ease if we don't rush or force them.

I absolutely loved my new school, and couldn't believe how different school morale was under the leadership of a caring, competent principal who led with her heart and valued her teachers highly.

Although she retired a year after I came to the school, her leadership was healing for me and helped restore my confidence. The tone she set in the school continued to reverberate through several cycles of administrators afterward, and I thrived there until the year I decided to pursue instructional coaching full time.

Soon after publishing the first edition of this book, a former colleague I'm still friendly with called to give me an update: *The principal who had micromanaged me was terminated in the middle of the school year.*

Though no one knew for sure what happened (as the district seemed to be covering up the scandal to avoid bad press), some internal documents that surfaced online claimed that the principal faced charges of mismanaging school funds and committing financial fraud.

My jaw dropped when I read this. So *that's* why he was always worried that I was doing something minor that would bring legal scrutiny on the school! *That's* why he wanted the paper trail of my apology letter for my website; *that's* why he didn't want "copyrighted for educational use" materials passed out in my parent workshop; *that's* why he was worried about me leaning against the fence at recess and not standing at attention in case a child got hurt!

I had an out-of-the-box teaching style, and didn't pay much attention to regulations that felt pointless to me...and that's a problem if you're a boss who's misappropriating funds in illegal ways and is terrified of having close scrutiny on your school.

I felt vindicated, of course, and it was a relief to have a fuller understanding of his motives. I'd be lying if I said I didn't experience some schadenfreude hearing that his career had gone down in flames.

But none of that changes the fact that I let this man make me miserable for nearly two years.

Restoring your peace, not the relationship

How much more would I have enjoyed teaching if I hadn't spent so much time complaining about him? How much more energy would I have had in the classroom if I'd refused to let him ruin my day with his petty demands?

That principal never had any idea how much mental torture I put myself through. It was me, not him, who suffered when I repeated to myself, *He SHOULD appreciate me! He SHOULD have a backbone and be a strong leader! He SHOULD stop micromanaging and let me teach!*

> **Holding a grudge doesn't weaken the person you resent, it weakens *you*.**

> **So, the main purpose of forgiving is not to pardon the other person, but to allow yourself to heal and move on. You are the primary beneficiary. Do it for your own peace of mind.**

It's also important to understand that forgiveness does not mean restoration. You do not have to allow the person who wronged you to resume the same place of trust and closeness as before.

I doubt that I would ever befriend my former principal or confide anything in him, should our paths cross again. That's not a necessary component of the forgiveness process, and would expose me to potential pain and betrayal.

When you forgive someone, you don't have to act as if nothing ever happened and try to return to the initial, untainted state of the relationship. But, you do need to stop thinking about what the person has done and quit holding it over their head.

In that sense, "forgive and forget" is pretty simple: stop thinking about it and stop talking about it. Dismiss, distract, reject, replace.

Forgiveness is not easy, but it's also not as complicated as we make it out to be. We often act as if there are all sorts of things that must happen before we can even think about forgiving someone.

A grudge can be weakened just by your refusal to keep it alive with your thoughts and conversations. If you don't allow yourself to entertain any thoughts about how the person has wronged you, the incident will fade from your memory, and the emotions attached to your thoughts will weaken.

How to think more forgiving thoughts

So, HOW do you forgive? Start from a place of curiosity rather than judgment. Stop repeating your unrealistic and irrational standards (*shoulds* and *musts*) in your mind.

What might be true about this person's motives or thought process that you haven't yet considered? See if you can mull over a few possibilities, and look for ways their behavior makes sense within the context of their separate realities.

Doing this naturally stirs up feelings of empathy: you've probably felt the same way they're feeling, and you haven't always made healthy choices, either. Actively decide to be merciful.

When you're tempted to compare other people's shortcomings to how they're "supposed to" behave, recognize what you're doing and replace those thoughts with healthier ones:

I'm choosing to forgive. The person who hurt me was probably responding from a place of hurt themselves. They were feeling insecure, angry, fearful, etc.

I'm upset not because of their actions, but because of how their actions conflict with my beliefs. Part of me thinks that I should always be treated fairly and kindly, and no one should ever hurt my feelings. But there is no law in the universe that says everyone will always treat me well, and clinging to that expectation will only cause me pain and misery.

A more accurate, rational belief is that sometimes, I will get hurt, and yet I will be okay. Imperfect people treat people imperfectly. This is not the end of the world. It's not worth upsetting myself over this. I'm choosing to think more rational thoughts because I know they will protect me from getting so stressed out in the future.

I'm going to choose to think thoughts of forgiveness. Whenever mean, judgmental thoughts pop up or I'm tempted to replay and rehearse conversations in my head, I'm going to dismiss those and replace them with positive thoughts. I will tell myself, "That person hurt me, but I've forgiven them. I'm not going to hold on to the pain anymore."

Decide to act from
your integrity and values

Just as you can refuse to let outside circumstances determine your thoughts and feelings, you can choose not to allow circumstances to determine your behavior.

You can act rather than react, and decide what your actions will be, regardless of what everyone else does. You don't have to anticipate problems or ruminate endlessly on what you'll do in particular scenarios. Just choose actions that are important to you and stick with them.

Creating healthy habits and routines

You might notice that when you pass by staff in the office, they sometimes speak and sometimes ignore you. That can leave you wondering each day, "Should I say hi? Should I ask how they're doing?" and wavering back and forth.

Instead, decide that you're going greet others in a way that's true to yourself every morning, regardless of how others respond. If you think it's nice for co-workers to acknowledge one another's presence, then decide that *you're* going to smile and say good morning to people. Don't wait to see whether someone else says hi and then determine whether or not to be friendly.

Then, when other people keep their heads down and don't greet you in return, refuse to take it personally and tell yourself, *Oh, well, I'm doing what I think is best here even if other people don't see things the same way. I'm not holding THEM to MY standards.*

Similarly, if you want to start each school day by making a personal connection with every student, make a decision to begin class that way as a regular routine.

Don't wait to see how the kids act or if you're in the mood to take time for it. Plant yourself in the doorway as kids are entering the room and connect with them.

Maybe you want to do positive outreach to parents and caregivers on occasion, instead of only contacting them when there's a problem. Stick with your plan!

If a bunch of phone numbers are disconnected, emails bounce back, and several parents act like there's something strange about you reaching out for no "real" reason, don't let their reactions discourage you.

The idea here is to avoid letting other people's behaviors set the tone or prevent you from showing up as the best version of yourself. Choose to move through your day in ways that you'll feel good about later, regardless of what everyone else is or isn't doing.

Stay solidly grounded in who you are, responding to other people in ways that are healthy and not overly influenced by their moods (or your own.)

The more you choose your actions ahead of time, the less reactive you'll be in the moment. This is an especially important practice for intuitives, empaths, and other folks who are highly attuned to the emotions of the people around them.

Act rather than react

It's easy to make good decisions when we're in a healthy mental state and a high mood. Little things don't bother us, and solutions seem clear.

In contrast, problems seem overwhelming and impossible when we're in reactive thinking patterns, and a low mood state is created. These are days in which it feels like everything is going wrong at once and we can't seem to catch a break.

Though it can feel like the universe is conspiring against you, the truth is that low, reactive mood states cause you to become easily agitated and decrease your tolerance for frustration.

It *seems* like more things are going wrong because your mood causes you to perceive minor setbacks as huge problems!

When you're in a good mood, having to wait for someone or give a student that third reminder seems like no big deal, and you don't upset yourself about it. But in a low mood, you enter a reactive state. You can easily become irritated, because you're mentally replaying how many things have gone wrong that day and insisting that the situation is "just one more thing" that you can't handle.

This is why it's so important to decide ahead of time how you want to act: you're choosing your behaviors when you're in a good mood. In that mind state, you can see the big picture and think long-term about the best course of action.

Then, when you experience a low mood and reactive state of mind, it's easier to behave wisely and in line with your character. You'll be able to step back from the situation and look on objectively, reminding yourself:

I'm not really having such a terrible day. I'm just in a "terrible" mood because I'm wallowing in my thoughts about how terrible things are! There's a big difference! I know there isn't as much pressure on me as I feel like there is today—it's just my low mood state that makes me feel like I can't handle as much at one time. I've got too many thoughts cluttering my head and I need to let some of them go. Then my frustration tolerance will rise back to my normal levels and I'll be able to handle problems better.

Selecting your behaviors when you're in a healthy mode of thinking sets you up to act rather than react during moments of stress. Your response to challenges will be based on who you really are, apart from the problems surrounding you. You'll be able to recognize when you're in a reactive mode and make better decisions about how to respond to setbacks.

Positive actions produce positive feelings

There's a behaviorist motto which says, "motivation often follows action." Most of us assume the opposite is true: we have to *feel like* doing something, and then we'll do it.

But sometimes, if we behave the way we want to feel, our positive actions will produce positive outcomes...and that in turn creates the happy, productive feelings we were waiting on.

Our thought patterns have a huge impact on the degree of difficulty we experience in making wise choices. If your mind repeats unrealistic standards and expectations, you're likely to get discouraged. If you jump to conclusions, over-generalize, and get sucked into false helplessness ("This isn't going to make a difference! There's no point in trying!"), it will be much harder to stay the course.

These types of thoughts will also create an emotional reaction, which makes it even tougher to choose your behaviors wisely. If you wait until you're angry, frustrated, depressed, exhausted, or in another strong emotional state, it will be much harder to select words and actions you'll be proud of later on.

Live in integrity and act on values, not feelings

One of my core values is to live in my own integrity: I don't want to sell out my own internal peace to keep someone else happy, or tell white lies as social glue to hold relationships together.

I want to show up as the same person no matter who I'm with, and be honest with other people about what I think and feel.

This means, for example, not telling people "I'm fine" when I'm not fine. Because I've given this a lot of consideration and reflected on how bad it makes me feel to pretend like everything is okay when it's not, I find it much easier to be honest in my interactions.

I no longer blurt out "Everything's good!" when people ask how I am. Instead, I take a moment to feel the answer in my body—how am I today, honestly? Then I find an answer that's aligned with how I truly feel and what's actually going on.

I might say, "Pretty good overall" or "Today's been a lot to deal with, but no major problems. How are you?"

If it's appropriate when I'm having a bad day, I might say, "I'm pretty tired today, and need to rest. I don't have a lot of bandwidth for anything additional."

This is a decision I made in advance: I'm not going to hide my struggles, tell other people want they want to hear, and disregard my real feelings. If I can't practice integrity in such a small moment (like truthfully answering the question, "How are you?") then how I will prepare to practice integrity when there's a bigger risk?

Another way to think of living with integrity is this: Don't act on your feelings; act on your values.

When you notice a strong emotion creeping in, you can choose to sit with it. You don't need to intellectualize it, judge it, or push it away. Just feel it.

And then, before acting on that feeling, cross reference it with your values.

Maybe you're so angry at someone that you feel like cussing them out or even hitting them. It's okay to feel angry. Having those thoughts cross your mind doesn't make you a bad person. You are not your thoughts; you are the watcher of your thoughts.

So, watch the thoughts come and go in your mind, attempting to be a neutral observer of them. Sit with the feelings that follow those thoughts.

When you're ready to choose an action, decide if it aligns with your values. If you're committed to treating others with kindness and compassion, act on those values, rather than the angry feelings.

Find satisfaction in the process

When you determine and commit to your behaviors ahead of time, this makes it easier to act on your values instead of on passing moods or the environment around you.

Make this part of your life-long practice with thought work, so that you don't feel guilty when you fall short of self-imposed expectations. Avoid creating unrealistic standards for yourself and getting discouraged when you fail to meet them ("I should always do this! I must be consistent!")

Instead, show grace toward yourself in moments of weakness when you slip into old patterns. You're establishing a mindset and a lifestyle, not creating a book of rules for yourself.

Sometimes you may wonder, *Why do I have to be the one who always does the right thing?*

Remind yourself: *Because I want the right results.*

Boost your energy and enthusiasm with thoughts like:

- *It feels good to do the right thing.*
- *I like how I feel when I take initiative instead of the easy way out.*
- *My actions make a difference whether I see it or not.*
- *Kindness and consideration on my part make it more likely that others will show those same traits.*
- *I'm being consistent with the advice I give my students: do the right thing even when no one's looking.*
- *Choosing these behaviors will make it easier for me to think peaceful thoughts and experience positive feelings. I'm training myself in ways that make me happier and more energetic.*

24

Embrace the path instead of perfectionism

It was official: I had 27 more days as a classroom teacher. I'd submitted my resignation and the final date was set. Instructional coaching and consulting were about to go from a side job to my full-time pursuit.

A mixture of emotions was brewing inside me—sadness, fear, excitement, relief.

But most of all, I was happy because I just *knew* I could be the perfect teacher for my last 27 days.

The coming weeks would hold a series of lasts: the last time I'd teach my favorite unit on ancient Egypt; the last time we'd make geometry flip books that ensured lines and angles would be something the kids looked forward to exploring; the last time I'd get to read aloud from my favorite children's books.

I wanted to do all of the activities and projects I'd intended to implement but ended up not doing because they were so energy intensive. Gingerbread house math! School-wide scavenger hunt! Class blog! Complete re-enactment of the food web in a student-written five-act play!

I also planned to be the model of patience and kindness for those last few weeks. I envisioned myself floating around the classroom, Queen of Benevolence, smiling wistfully when kids were off-task and gratefully seizing every conflict as an opportunity to model social problem solving.

And yet somehow I was showing up as the worst version of myself.

I was distracted by the long distance move ahead and my latest consulting contract, which I'd already started. Once again, the kids were somehow in my way. Rather than treasuring every second, I began to resent them: *Seriously, I've got three weeks left, they can't walk in a quiet line without pushing each other for three weeks?*

For the first time in years, I started coming home in a bad mood almost every day. My husband just couldn't figure it out. "Honey, you've only got these kids for a few more days. Why are you letting them get to you? Where is all this frustration coming from?"

I couldn't quite explain that I had raised the bar for both myself and the students.

I was expecting a perfection that none of us had ever demonstrated before. Yet I thought that putting a time limit on how long we would need to be perfect would somehow make that possible.

I'd love to tell you that in my final weeks as a classroom teacher, I had fully realized all the concepts in this book and was the picture of grace and long suffering.

But I was (and am) still a work in progress; an educator who falls short, makes mistakes, and feels regret. When I look back now on that time in my life, I realize that I expected far too much.

Being awakened is the initial realization of truth, the moment when the light illuminates a situation and you can see it clearly for the first time. Growth begins there, but a true awakening is a process. It's a daily decision to choose thoughts that help you feel the way you want to feel. Expecting perfection will only create disappointment and frustration.

Viewing setbacks as opportunities

Perhaps while reading this book, you had a moment or series of moments in which you felt you were awakened to truth and new possibilities.

You could sense that you'd been going through life in a sleepwalk, oblivious to how much you were existing in darkness, and now you are alert and aware of the potential to enjoy your work and your life in a deeper way.

I encourage you to continue on the path of awakening by viewing each setback as a chance to know yourself better, and more fully embody the truest version of who you are.

An awakening is not some super-spiritual goal that is only achieved by meditating in a silent retreat for months at a time. Mundane tasks and minor inconveniences are often the best way to learn.

When you're running late in the morning, you have the chance to practice having flexible expectations.

When a colleague is rude, you have an occasion to believe the best and practice forgiveness.

Every time you feel agitated or upset, you can interpret the situation as an opportunity for personal growth.

And each time you respond to problems in a healthy way, you've made it easier for yourself to respond that way again in the future. It's like you're immunizing yourself against future stress. You're building up a tolerance for frustration. You're training yourself not to get so upset or bothered by problems.

When you hold this perspective, setbacks that just keep coming one after another can seem almost comical. You can step back and detach from the problems. The issues you're facing feel less overwhelming, because you see them within the big picture and acknowledge how they can work to your benefit in the long run.

You won't always be able to view things this way, of course. When you start to feel discouraged about the way you handled a stressful situation, remind yourself that you've already conquered the hardest part: awareness.

Many people go their entire lives without recognizing the effects of their negative thought patterns. Be *glad* that you see something wrong with your thinking and reactions—your awareness is what will allow you to choose your thoughts with more intentionality.

In fact, the phase of self-development in which you can observe yourself making mistakes is an important one. It's the bridge from your old self (which was oblivious to harmful thought patterns) to your highest self (which is well-established in healthy thought patterns.)

So when you feel yourself slipping into a negative thought spiral, don't say, "I know better than this! I promised myself I wouldn't do that again. I can't believe I'm still struggling!"

Instead, your self-talk might sound like this:

I'm glad I recognized what was happening before too much damage was caused. In the past, I would have wallowed in this for days or even weeks. The fact that I only followed that negative train of thought for an hour is quite an improvement! My thinking patterns are getting more and more healthy.

Self-compassion is so important. There's a good chance that, at times, other people will not be particularly supportive and appreciative of either your teaching or your efforts toward self-improvement.

Practice showing support to *yourself.* Compliment yourself on a job well done. Incorporate praise into your self-talk: *Woo-hoo, awesome work! Getting better all the time!*

Be as encouraging to yourself as you are to your students when they make mistakes: *You can do it! Try again! Don't give up now!*

You can do anything, but you cannot do everything

I think a lot of us assume that if we teach long enough, there will come a time in our careers in which we'll manage everything on our plates with ease. One day, we'll get all the district's paperwork done on time or early, return graded work to students within twenty-four hours (with individualized comments, of course), and have detailed lesson plans completed at least a week in advance. The pressure will finally be off once we become a "master teacher."

This might be the most damaging myth that teachers ever believe. I have to break the news: you will never be at a place where you can sit back and say, "Great! There's nothing left for me to do. My classroom is perfect and all of my students' needs are met 100% of the time!"

You will *never* be able to do it all as well as you'd like to. You will *never* be able to do everything the district tells you to as well as you'd like to do it.

Let that really sink in. Does your principal effectively and efficiently complete everything the teachers, students, parents, and superintendent ask? Do district officials do everything they're supposed to, perfectly and on time?

Of course not. They're under intense pressure from all sides, just like you. They, too, are asked to do the impossible. *And they don't.*

So why should you berate YOURSELF for not being a miracle worker? Everyone around you is just doing the best they can with what they've got. You should, too.

In education, the standards are high and the stakes are higher. So no matter how efficient you become, there will not be enough hours in the day to meet every demand that's placed on you.

And still, the world will not come to an end. You don't have to hold yourself to an unachievable standard.

Productivity expert David Allen phrases it this way: "You can do anything, but you cannot do everything." Set your efforts on what's most important, and don't let yourself feel discouraged about not being Super Teacher.

I found it helpful to focus on improving in one major area during each school year. I developed monthly parent-caregiver workshops one year and planned ways to strengthen my communication and relationships with families. Another year, I read every book I could find on Writer's Workshop and developed a huge repertoire of best practices for writing instruction. Another year I created backward planning units for science to make sure I was teaching kids the big ideas and essential questions.

Each fall, I'd keep up the practices I'd learned from the previous years and embark on a new area of improvement.

Then when I noticed that I was weak in a particular area, rather than criticize myself, I could say, *That's a good area of professional development to consider for next year. One focus at a time. I can't become an expert in every teaching practice all at once, and I'm not going to pressure myself. I'm aware that I have learning to do in this area, and that's a good first step. I'll get better and better at this the longer I'm in the profession.*

Letting go of unhappiness

The responsibility of teaching brings with it the potential for an endless amount of personal satisfaction and deeply rewarding experiences.

But that can't be the prerequisite for our happiness.

Though the good times are re-energizing, it's unrealistic to expect that *every* moment in the classroom will match your best ones.

If you're easily discouraged because you can't replicate your biggest success with another class or another lesson, you risk getting frustrated because you aren't seeing the results you think you "should" have. You miss out on the emotional high that comes from a rewarding moment when you wish that things could be that fantastic all the time.

And when you're at a low point, you lose what little energy you have left by looking backward (or forward) and comparing. Your mind is consumed with thoughts like, *Last year's class was so much nicer* and *I hope next year's class catches on to things more quickly*. The present moment slips away, simply because you haven't chosen to enjoy your work right now, exactly as it is.

Wishing we could sleep later, wishing students would behave, wishing the school system would have different priorities…we expend so much energy on how things might be, could be, should be.

This causes us to miss out on the little daily instances of happiness because we are so busy in our *pursuit* of happiness.

We don't realize that satisfaction is not a future goal we can work toward. It is here right now, if we choose to experience it. Though we cannot be happy all the time, we can cultivate a lifestyle of gratitude by being mindful in the present moment.

Neither happiness nor contentment are end goals. They are by-products of a life lived with consciousness and awareness.

The process of learning to enjoy your job is more about letting go of unhappiness than striving toward happiness. It's about learning to release unrealistic standards, expectations, demands on the moment, and cognitive distortions. And above all, it's about letting go of the thoughts that are taking away your good feelings.

As you rid your mind of thoughts that create suffering, you'll uncover a state of mind that is relaxed and calm.

I was astonished when I discovered that my true self—the one that was buried underneath all those bad mental habits, childhood and family patterns, learned behaviors, cognitive biases, emotional baggage, and trauma—was actually very peaceful and content.

I genuinely began to like myself and enjoy my own company. Being in my own head was a truly pleasant experience. I had so much more energy and enthusiasm for daily life when I wasn't burdened with worry and controlling tendencies.

I encourage you to pursue your awakening with passion. Enjoy the process! Look forward to learning new lessons about yourself. Have a sense of humor about making mistakes and going through the trial-and-error process.

Envision yourself stripping away all of the cognitive habits that don't serve you well, until the real you—the person you truly are at your core—is totally uncovered.

Each day will bring more opportunities to practice letting go of stress-creating perceptions and allow contentment, peace, and joy to be revealed.

Your new mindset will open you up to all kinds of possibilities that you didn't have the ability to dream before. Take satisfaction in this, and let every part of your teaching and your life be transformed by the renewing of your mind.

Afterword:
The self-talk of an awakened teacher

So how does all this advice fit together, and what does it look like when applied to daily life?

Here are some examples of how you can use the *Awakened* principles to construct positive, resilient self-talk throughout the school day:

5:30 am: Dreading having to get up and go to work

It's okay for me to feel tired today. I don't have to pay attention to the thoughts about how exhausted I am: I can just notice those thoughts and let them pass. I'm setting my intent: I accept whatever comes my way and trust that I can handle it. Today I'm going to act rather than react, have flexible expectations, and practice keeping a healthy state of mind.

7:35: A colleague called in sick and there's no substitute; eight of her students will be placed in your class

Hmm, okay. That throws a wrench in my plans, but at least the office told me before school started so I could have materials ready for her students. I can choose to repeat my expectation that this should not be happening, or I can accept it and deal with it. This is the reality today, and I have work to do, so I'm not going to get caught up in how unfair the situation is right now. After school, I can decide if and when I want to address it with my principal—for now, I'm focusing on the kids.

7:45: Parent calls and complains about something minor

The most important thing I can do is communicate to this parent that I care about his child's progress. This parent needs reassurance that I'm doing everything I can to support his child. I'm going to choose empathy and show patience toward him. I'm believing the best about his intentions. That's how I'd want my child's teacher to treat me.

8:00: Students burst into the classroom yelling and pushing

This is not the way I've trained students to treat each other or our learning environment. Rather than start my day by getting angry, I'm going to take a deep breath, and calmly ask them to go back out and come back in the way we've practiced. I'm not taking this as a personal affront; they were just wound up from the bus ride. My goal is not to punish, but to support them in learning appropriate behaviors. I can handle this calmly rather than matching their chaotic energy. This incident is not going to set the wrong tone for the day.

8:25: Seven students have not completed their morning bell work

This is disappointing, but not unbelievable. It's irrational to think that all students should complete all their work 100% of the time. I can't even meet that standard myself—I scrolled through social media last night instead of getting my own tasks done! So I'm not going to let this discourage or irritate me, and I won't make judgments about the kids' motives or anticipate problems with this in the future. I'm going to handle it in this moment, and mentally move on.

9:07: Classroom phone and intercom have buzzed six times during an important lesson

Ugh, so annoying! Better not waste any MORE time by thinking about how much I hate interruptions. Otherwise I'll be on edge and probably lose my temper with the next person who interrupts class, and that's not fair to them. We have a staff meeting later this week and I can address the issue then. For now, I don't want to distract myself further...back to the lesson!

9:45: Discover that a colleague has borrowed materials without permission

This is the third time she's done this. I can get myself riled up about it, or choose thoughts that feel less reactive. I'll ask her not to do that again, but I won't rehearse the conversation in my mind repeatedly beforehand. And, I'm going to be aware of the story I'm telling myself about her, because I don't want to harbor resentment and jeopardize our working relationship which is really important to me. Why should I waste time trying to figure out why she acts the way she does, or complain about it to other teachers? I'll talk to her and set my boundaries, and then move on.

10:15: The district does a surprise walk-through evaluation

Wow, I was not expecting this! I sure would have liked for this person to arrive five minutes earlier when we were doing a more rigorous activity. Oh well, it is what it is! I'm not going to panic and worry about what that person thought. My students were working on a planned part of the lesson that was necessary for their learning, even if it wasn't impressive to an outside observer. I know I'm doing my job to the best of my ability, and I'm proud of my efforts. My self-confidence doesn't come from what a stranger says after spending two minutes in my classroom.

10:38: Student refuses to do any work, interrupts your instruction constantly, and gets an attitude when you correct him—AGAIN

I refuse to let this child's behavior cause me to hate my job or assume my whole day is ruined. I'm not giving him that power. This is his reality, and these are his choices. He'll have to deal with the consequences that we've already worked out together, and I don't have to see that as a personal problem for me. I can choose to respond in calm, compassionate ways that help him emotionally regulate and get back on task. It won't be easy or fun, but I CAN respond constructively, and I will! I have this kid for ten months out of my lifetime. I can deal with anything for ten months.

11:04: Paraprofessional is late to teach her small group

This has happened before, so I may need to set more realistic expectations here. I'd love for her to be on time, but I can't control what another adult does. And, I know from our past conversations that it's tough for her to wrap up a small group in Ms. Smith's classroom all the way on the other side of the building, and get over here to begin teaching immediately afterward with no break. I'm going to just accept the reality that she's often a couple minutes late, and plan accordingly so my class' schedule isn't thrown off. I'm going to get the rest of the class settled in their activity, and train the group who's waiting for the para to read books together quietly until she arrives. That way the kids aren't just sitting around wasting time, and they're ready to begin as soon as she's here. This isn't worth getting upset or indignant about. I'm certainly not on time for everything, either.

11:45: Co-workers are complaining in the faculty lounge during lunch

I'm tuning out and then changing the subject as soon as I can find a good opening. There's no point in reinforcing those negative thoughts that I, too, have about students sometimes—I'll just be impatient with the kids all afternoon if I listen to this. Oh, here comes someone else, I'll start a conversation with them! Perfect. We've both been streaming that new TV series and I want to hear their opinion of the latest episode.

12:00 pm: Photocopier is jammed

Gahhh, now I won't have the papers I need for this afternoon's lesson! I'm tempted to over-generalize here and get into a rant about how I NEVER have the materials I need and nothing in this building EVER works, but I don't want to carry that stress with me. I can just smirk and shake my head—it's actually kind of comical how fast things break around here! I'm defusing my frustration by finding humor in the situation, and I'm going to focus my attention on creating an alternative plan of action. Let's see, if I won't have these copies, what can I do with students instead?

12:05: Discover that two students got in a fight during lunch and are down in the office

Well, that's disappointing. I'm glad it didn't happen under my watch, though, and the kids are already in the principal's office discussing it. I'll shut down any gossip among the rest of the class and get them focused on the warm-up. After school I'll talk to the principal. Until then, I'm not going to jump to any conclusions about who's at fault, or speculate about what happened. I don't have to hold this issue in my mind or interpret it as a problem. It's not my concern at the moment, and I'll handle it when I have more information.

1:17: Working with a student who is just not getting the concept

I've tried everything I can think of to help this kid—it's so frustrating that things still aren't clicking into place! But if I get upset, then I've got two problems to deal with: his lack of understanding, and my emotional reaction. It's unrealistic for me to expect all students to understand these concepts at the pace the curriculum demands. They're humans, not machines, and each individual progresses on their own developmental timeline. This child needs more time and different types of practice. I can let go of the assumption that this is a problem. There's nothing wrong with him OR me: this is a normal part of the learning process, which happens at different rates.

2:20: Assistant principal emails and asks to see you after school

Uh-oh—what did I do? Did a parent call to complain? Could this be about...no, wait. There's no need to jump to conclusions and assume the worst. She probably just wants to fill me in on the fight in the cafeteria at lunch. Chances are, this is not something terrible and I'm not in trouble. I'm going to put this out of my head until it's time to deal with it. It's just not helpful or useful for me to expend any mental energy trying to figure out what she wants to talk about. I've still got kids to teach for another half hour! Back to work.

3:00: Boring, pointless committee meeting

There doesn't seem to be anything I can learn from this meeting. Maybe I can shift my focus to adding value. Is there something useful I can contribute? Do I have any advice or experiences that would help? Do I have any suggestions that could speed the process up a bit? Is there someone here that looks like they need encouragement? Might as well set my own purpose for the meeting so it's not a total waste!

4:00: Need to leave school to get to an appointment, but have so many things left to do

As much as I hate to leave now, I accept that I've done everything I can do today. Rather than focus on all the things I left undone, I'm going to walk to my car and make a mental list of everything I accomplished. Let's see...I talked to my assistant principal and everything is fine—I wasn't in trouble, and I'm so glad I didn't stress and worry about it all afternoon! I got my grades entered into the computer; that was a relief. I made a connection with my new student during reading instruction, I helped Mr. Lamont troubleshoot his printer, we finally got started on the solar system project...oh, and I figured out how to help Marcus understand the difference between adjectives and adverbs! This was actually a very productive day! Let me see what other good things I can recall...

6:45: Eating dinner; worried about a student's personal and home life

I can't control what's happening at students' homes, and upsetting myself with speculation only ruins my own dinner—it doesn't make things better for the kids. I have alerted the guidance counselor and made sure the family service worker is checking in regularly. I made time during the school day to connect with the student and monitor how things are going. I've already done what I can do for this student today. In this moment, the only thing I need to do is be present with my own family and enjoy the meal we're sharing. That way I won't be worn down and emotionally drained tomorrow when I'm with my students again.

8:20: Feeling resentful about finishing data entry work

I really don't want to be doing this right now. But there's no law of life that guarantees I only get to do fun things in my evenings. Though I don't like it, I accept that sometimes I need to bring work home in order to prepare properly for the next day. It will be easier to get this task done if I don't repeat to myself how much I hate it and wish I didn't have to do it. Once the data is entered, I shouldn't need to work in the evenings for a while. Plus, I've already made the decision not to work at all over the weekend. I'm being very intentional with my time, and not just bringing home tons of school stuff unnecessarily. This is an important task, and as soon as it's done, I'm going to relax.

10:45: Tired but not ready to sleep; worrying about a parent conference in the morning

I don't feel like going to bed now—I just want to lay here and scroll on my phone for a bit longer. But, I'm going to choose to override my mood and make a healthier choice. The best thing I can do for myself right now is get a good night's rest so I'll be fresh in the morning. I don't know how the conference is going to go, but I trust that I'll say and do the right thing when the time comes. *I've written down my key points so I can let it go for right now. The only thing I need to do is rest tonight, and eat a healthy breakfast in the morning. I trust that my inner wisdom will surface when I need it. Whatever happens tomorrow, I know I'll be able to handle it!*

Recommended Resources

I've created a comprehensive list of authors, educators, and other experts who have informed my work and serve as further reading recommendations.

If you would like to dig deeper into positive psychology, CBT, DBT, ACT, mindfulness, or any other approaches from this book, please visit: www.TruthForTeachers.com/awakened.

There you'll find a continually updated list of links to recommended books, websites, and the social media handles of folks you can learn from.

Stay Connected

Here are some other ways to keep learning and get new ideas and resources about the topics from this book:

- Subscribe to my Truth for Teachers podcast for inspiring audio messages
- Sign up for weekly encouragement and strategies via email
- Follow me on Instagram, Twitter, Facebook, or TikTok
- Inquire about having me speak or conduct PD at your school

I would love for you to reach out via social media or email and introduce yourself. There's nothing that inspires my work more than hearing from teachers who are determined to create change and think outside the box. You've heard my story — now it's time to tell yours!

Go to TruthforTeachers.com/awakened to access all the resources and contact methods listed here.

About the Author

ANGELA WATSON is a National Board Certified Teacher with a master's degree in Curriculum and Instruction. She has 11 years of classroom experience and over a decade of experience as an instructional coach and educational consultant.

Angela created her website in 2003 (now called TruthForTeachers.com) to share practical classroom ideas and help other educators build a positive mindset so they can truly enjoy their work. She has authored numerous printable curriculum resources, online courses, and six books (three of which are currently in print).

She is perhaps best known for her free Truth for Teachers podcast, which consistently ranks in the top K-12 podcasts in the world, and provides weekly encouragement for educators.

Angela's productivity professional development is used in tens of thousands of schools through the 40 Hour Workweek program. 40 Hour is designed to help teachers, instructional coaches, and school administrators be intentional with their time so they can focus on what really matters. Educators who utilize the 40 Hour principles can find a sustainable approach to their jobs, maximizing their contractual time so they're not working endlessly on nights and weekends.

Through Angela's mentorship, countless educators have learned to take charge of their time and energy so they can prevent burnout and stay in the profession they love for years to come.